Nuclear Weapons
A comprehensive study

United Nations Department for Disarmament Affairs

Nuclear Weapons
A comprehensive study

United Nations, New York, 1991

United Nations Publications
United Nations, Room DC2–0853
New York, New York 10017, USA

United Nations Publications
Palais des Nations
1211 Geneva 10, Switzerland

United Nations Sales No. E.91.IX.10
ISBN 92-1-142172-1

Preface

In 1988 the United Nations General Assembly adopted resolution 43/75N, in which it requested the Secretary-General to update the 1980 comprehensive study on nuclear weapons. The Secretary-General assembled a group of experts from 12 countries, which prepared the report between March 1989 and July 1990.

The present study represents the most comprehensive review of the relevant developments in this field over the past decade or so. It also covers recent events which were unfolding while the Group of Experts was finalizing the text of the study. Thus, the study deals in its analyses with the documents adopted at the summit meetings of the Warsaw Treaty Organization and NATO held in June and July 1990 respectively, which contain statements of political and military significance for the entire range of issues related to nuclear weapons and strategic doctrines. The study moreover takes into account the results of the summit meeting held between President Bush of the United Sates and President Gorbachev of the Soviet Union in June 1990 in Washington, at which important agreements in principle were reached for significant reductions in strategic offensive nuclear forces of the two nuclear-weapon Powers.

The study contains several significant conclusions. One of them is that the quantitative growth of nuclear-weapon arsenals has been stopped. The total number of nuclear warheads in the world has declined and this trend is expected to continue. The danger of nuclear confrontation has been significantly reduced if not eliminated altogether. On the other hand, however, qualitative improvements of nuclear-weapon systems, though confined to several areas, continue without significant restrictions. The question of the cessation of nuclear-weapon tests remains a highly divisive issue in international discussions.

In his foreword, the Secretary-General of the United Nations, Javier Pérez de Cuéllar, observed that to his mind, while disarmament negotiations regarding nuclear weapons are generally moving in the right direction and, as a result, a nuclear danger is less pronounced today than was the case a decade ago, the main task of the international community in the present realities in international relations remains threefold:

- to preserve resolutely the present positive momentum in the negotiations for the reduction of nuclear weapons, with a view to their eventual complete elimination;
- to find ways and means of effectively curbing the continued qualitative improvements in this field; and
- to strengthen the barriers against possible proliferation of nuclear weapons to non-nuclear-weapon States.

With the process of nuclear disarmament finally begun, it would be against the interests of international peace and security if new nuclear-weapon States should now emerge, just as would be the case if the nuclear-weapons States should fail to capitalize on the positive momentum in international relations to achieve further substantive agreements.

The Group of Experts participating in the study were as follows: Ambassador Mohamed El-Shaffei Abdel Hamid of Egypt, Mr. Gustavo Ainchil of Argentina, Mr. Alexander Akalovsky of the United States of America, Mr. Gilles Curien of France, Dr. Radoslav Deyanov of Bulgaria, Dr. Hedy Hernández of Venezuela, Ambassador Brett Lineham of New Zealand, Mr. H. M. G. S. Palihakkara of Sri Lanka, Ambassador Nana Sutresna of Indonesia, Mr. Cheikh Sylla of Senegal, Ambassador Maj Britt Theorin of Sweden (Chairman), and Professor Henry A. Trofimenko of the Union of Soviet Socialist Republics. A list of the members of the Group indicating their affiliation is contained in appendix III.

The Department for Disarmament Affairs, acting on behalf of the Secretary-General, assisted the Group of Experts in the preparation of the report.

Contents

I
Introduction

On 7 December 1988, the General Assembly adopted resolution 43/75 N, the operative paragraphs of which read as follows:

"*The General Assembly,*

"...

"1.   *Requests* the Secretary-General to carry out, with the assistance of qualified governmental experts[1] and taking into account recent relevant studies, a comprehensive update of the *Comprehensive Study on Nuclear Weapons* that provides factual and up-to-date information on and pays regard to the political, legal and security aspects of:

(*a*)   Nuclear arsenals and pertinent technological developments;

(*b*)   Doctrines concerning nuclear weapons;

(*c*)   Efforts to reduce nuclear weapons;

(*d*)   Physical, environmental, medical and other effects of use of nuclear weapons and of nuclear testing;

(*e*)   Efforts to achieve a comprehensive nuclear-test ban;

(*f*)   Efforts to prevent the use of nuclear weapons and their horizontal and vertical proliferation;

(*g*)   The question of verification of compliance with nuclear-arms limitation agreements;

"2.   *Recommends* that the study, while aiming at being as comprehensive as possible, should be based on open material and such further information as Member States may wish to make available for the purpose of the study;

"3.   *Invites* all Governments to co-operate with the Secretary-General so that the objectives of the study may be achieved;

"4.   *Requests* the Secretary-General to submit the final report to the General Assembly well in advance of its forty-fifth session."

The update of the 1980 study[2] has been prepared against the background of important changes that have occurred in international relations in the last 10 years since its publication. They are characterized by the global quantitative and continued qualitative developments of nuclear weapons on the one hand and major breakthroughs in arms limitation and disarmament negotiations on the other.

On the technical level, research, development, production and deployment of new weapons have continued steadily, with the attendant introduction of more accurate nuclear ballistic missile systems and the deployment of highly accurate nuclear-armed cruise missiles. Accuracy, low yield and miniaturization led to MIRVed (MIRV — multiple independently targetable re-entry vehicle) intercontinental ballistic missiles (ICBMs) and the development of new types of cruise missiles — whether sea-, air- or land-launched — at relatively limited costs. The possibility of ballistic missile defence (BMD) technologies based on various concepts is also being explored.

In reviewing these developments, the study refers to figures, estimates and other data based on various open academic and other non-governmental sources. Some data are, however, officially published by nuclear-weapon States, though such information is generally classified. The Governments of the respective nuclear-weapon States do not necessarily concur with the data given by non-official sources.

In 1990 there are about 50,000 nuclear warheads deployed around the world on the territories of the nuclear-weapon States and some non-nuclear-weapon States, as well as on the high seas. Each of the two major Powers has at least 10,000 nuclear warheads, which can be set into action in a major strategic attack within minutes or hours.

The possibility of the development of nuclear weapons by additional States also continues to be a deep concern. The Fourth Review Conference of the Treaty on the Non-Proliferation of Nuclear Weapons will take place at Geneva from 20 August to 14 September 1990. It is the last one before 1995, when a Conference will be held to decide whether the Treaty shall continue in force indefinitely, or shall be extended for an additional fixed period or periods. In addition, there have been recent reports of more countries developing short- and intermediate-range ballistic missiles. These issues may be expected to gain rising attention in the forthcoming months and years of the new decade.

The end of the 1980s may have heralded an end to the cold war and the cresting of an escalating arms race that has prevailed for the 45 years since the Second World War. The growing *rapprochement* between East and West, movement towards settlement of various regional conflicts, important political changes in Europe and other regions of the world and the increasing involvement of the United Nations in major issues facing the international community create favourable opportunities for the pursuit of meaningful measures in arms limitation and disarmament. Indeed, major progress has been made in several areas, both bilaterally between the United States and the Soviet Union and between members of the North Atlantic Treaty Organization and the Warsaw Treaty Organization. Although global stability and peace have not yet been attained, positive developments in international relations continue to gain momentum. These positive trends do not remove the need to continue the urgent search for solutions to regional problems in Asia and Africa so as to preclude the possibility of a conflict and, in particular, to prevent the use of weapons of mass destruction should a conflict nevertheless occur. This matter and its impact on global stability should be accorded the utmost importance.

In the same decade the first agreement providing for actual reductions in nuclear weapons, the Treaty between the United States of America and the Union of Soviet Socialist Republics on the Elimination of Their Intermediate-Range and Shorter-Range Missiles (INF Treaty), was signed in 1987. It provides for the elimination of a whole category of nuclear weapons under a system of unprecedented intrusive verification. This Treaty has paved the way for further progress on other arms limitation agreements.

The nuclear arms race may be turned around by the strategic offensive arms reduction treaty (START), the basic provisions of which were agreed to by the Soviet Union and the United States in June 1990. The international community has welcomed the agreement on the framework for such a treaty — which will reduce the Soviet and United States strategic nuclear weapons by approximately 30 to 35 per cent — as contributing to global security and as a step towards nuclear disarmament.

The continued improvement in international relations, particularly between the two major Powers, the levelling off of the quantitative increases in the nuclear-weapon arsenals, and the prospects for deep cuts all point to positive trends towards a less dangerous world. Although qualitative improvements in nuclear weapons continue and nuclear testing remains a contentious issue, the diminishing tension and the growing co-operation between East and West might facilitate the resolution of these issues as well. However, the possibility of the proliferation of nuclear weapons to additional States is of increasing concern. Some believe that the current political climate presents opportunities for taking steps that would minimize the chance or effect of possible untoward developments in the future.

Notes

1. Subsequently referred to as the Group of Governmental Experts to Carry Out a Comprehensive Update of the Study on Nuclear Weapons.

2. United Nations publication (Sales No. E.81.I.11). The study was subsequently reprinted in *Nuclear Weapons. Report of the Secretary-General*, Cambridge, Massachusetts, Autumn Press, 1981.

II
Existing nuclear weapons:
Technical data and statistics[1]

A.
Introduction

Nuclear weapons represent a historically new form of weaponry, which, by their multiple and far-reaching effects, provide a means of warfare whose mass destructive potential is unparalleled in human experience. Nuclear technology makes it possible to release more energy in one micro-second from a single nuclear weapon than all the energy released by conventional weapons used in all wars throughout history. In addition, nuclear weapons differ from conventional ones by the nature of their destructive effects, which comprise three elements: blast, heat and radiation. While the blast and heat are of an instantaneous nature, the radiation, which is peculiar to nuclear weapons, has both immediate and long-term effects. These effects have the potential to extend to areas beyond the borders of the target country.

The exact number of nuclear weapons in the world is difficult to estimate precisely. It seems that the current global total of nuclear warheads may be about 50,000, despite the elimination of some missile systems resulting from the 1987 INF Treaty between the United States and the Soviet Union. The 1980 United Nations study on nuclear weapons placed the total at that time in excess of 40,000. This would imply a significant quantitative increase. However, there are numerous indications that the 1980 estimate was too low. Consequently, the current figure of 50,000 may actually represent a decrease in the number of warheads.

The individual explosive yield of currently deployed nuclear warheads is estimated to span the spectrum from 100 tons to more than 1 million tons equivalent of conventional high explosive. In the 1970s and early 1980s the trend was towards deploying nuclear warheads of smaller individual yields that had a greater accuracy in their delivery. Even with this trend the aggregate explosive power of present nuclear arsenals remains in the region of 13,000 million tons of TNT, or 1 million times the explosive energy of the Hiroshima atomic bomb.[2]

There are five States that have officially acknowledged that they possess nuclear weapons: China, France, the Soviet Union, the United Kingdom and the United States. According to the figures given by the Stockholm International Peace Research Institute (SIPRI), the nuclear arsenals of the Soviet Union and the United States continue to contain more than 95 per cent of the total number of nuclear weapons in the world (see figure 1).

B.
Short description of physical properties of nuclear weapons

The essential part of a nuclear weapon is the nuclear explosive device or warhead. Warheads may be built into various kinds of missiles, gravity bombs, artillery shells and so on. The term "nuclear weapon" usually denotes both the nuclear warhead and the delivery vehicle that takes the warhead to the target, particularly when this vehicle is a missile. Over the years, both warheads and delivery vehicles have undergone significant processes of development and improvement (see chap. III). A "nuclear-weapon system" may include specially designed platforms, from which weapons are launched, as well as supportive systems for command, control and so on.

1.
Nuclear warheads

There are two basic types of nuclear warheads: those based solely on fission (previously often called atomic weapons) and those which also utilize fusion (sometimes called thermonuclear or hydrogen weapons). The energy released in a nuclear explosion (yield) is usually measured in kilotons (kt) or megatons (Mt) corresponding to the energy released by a thousand or a million metric tons of the conventional explosive TNT (trinitrotoluene).[3]

In a fission weapon, uranium or plutonium nuclei are split into lighter fragments — fission products. If there is more than a certain minimum amount of fissile material — the critical mass — a chain reaction can be initiated.[4] Conventional high explosives are used to bring the critical mass together very quickly to enable it to explode with great force. For a plutonium bomb the fissile material may be put together to a size that may be no larger in volume than a human fist.

In a fusion weapon, the nuclei of heavy hydrogen isotopes — deuterium and tritium — are fused together at very high temperatures.

Figure 1. *Estimated distribution of strategic nuclear arsenals (warheads and bombs) of the United States of America and the Union of Soviet Socialist Republics*

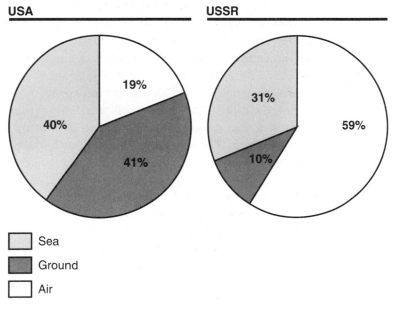

USA

USSR

19%

40%

41%

31%

10%

59%

Sea

Ground

Air

Source: SIPRI

The fusion process is triggered by a fission explosion. The fission device is indispensable as a triggering mechanism for thermonuclear explosions.[5]

The energy released by a thermonuclear weapon (H-bomb) comes from both the fission "trigger" and the fusion materials. However, the amount of energy released per kilogram of nuclear explosive material can be several times as large from a fusion device as from a fission device. Extra fission energy can be added by surrounding the fusion weapons with a shell of uranium-238. The greater the proportion of fission energy released the "dirtier" the thermonuclear weapon becomes. It is called "dirty" because of the quantity of highly radioactive substances (e.g. strontium-90 and caesium-137) that are released into the atmosphere. "Cleaner" weapons have a much smaller release of these substances.

2.
Characteristics of nuclear warhead materials

All nuclear weapons contain at least a few kilograms of weapon-grade plutonium or highly enriched uranium — the fissile material. Tritium is used in all thermonuclear warheads (hydrogen bombs). Tritium, like plutonium, does not occur in nature in extractable quantities and must be created in nuclear reactors. Plutonium decays with a half-life of about 24,000 years, which means it can be stored, whereas tritium has a half-life of 12 years, and therefore requires continuous production.

Natural uranium is composed of two main isotopes: 0.7 per cent is uranium-235, which is a fissile isotope, and 99.3 per cent is uranium-238, which requires high neutron energies to fission. In order to create nuclear weapons, the percentage of uranium-235 present in the uranium must be increased substantially. There are many ways to increase the percentage of uranium-235, the most common being gaseous diffusion.[6]

The majority of nuclear weapons developed in the world today use plutonium-239 (produced by neutron irradiation of uranium-238), rather than uranium-235, as fissionable material. Plutonium-239 is easily split in a fission process. A production line for plutonium requires the capability to refine — but not necessarily to enrich — uranium, the fabrication of reactor fuel, a nuclear reactor and a chemical plant for plutonium extraction from the spent fuel elements (reprocessing).[7]

3.

Delivery vehicles

The most important delivery vehicles for nuclear weapons are different types of rocket or jet-propelled missiles. There is, however, a variety of nuclear weapons that are designed to be delivered on targets by other means, e.g. gravity bombs, artillery shells, torpedoes and depth charges.

Missiles can be divided into different categories according to several criteria, such as by range, by means of propulsion, by basing mode or by notions of possible use. Long-range land-based and sea-based delivery vehicles are mainly ballistic missiles, while cruise missiles are important at somewhat shorter ranges.

A ballistic missile is a pilotless rocket-propelled projectile. It consists of one or more fuel stages and the final stage, which is sometimes called the warhead. The term "ballistic" derives from the motion of the final stage, which is governed by inertia and gravity after separation from the rocket.

Long-range missiles of this kind through vertical trajectory are capable of reaching outer space and travelling long distances before re-entering the atmosphere and reaching the target; hence the term "re-entry vehicle" (RV). The final stage may contain several nuclear warheads, which are then to be regarded as separate re-entry vehicles. In this case, the final stage is often called the "bus". The final stage may also contain various penetration aids, such as decoys (devices that resemble nuclear warheads on radar screens and are designed to confuse defences against in-coming missiles).

Multiple RVs, which are released from the bus as soon as possible, follow separate ballistic trajectories for most of their flight paths. MRVs are not independently targeted but fall within a given diameter surrounding the target. Multiple independently targeted re-entry vehicles (MIRVs) can be independently aimed to impact upon different targets.

An important characteristic of ballistic missiles is the so-called throw-weight. This refers to the maximum weight of the useful load (warhead, guidance unit and penetration aids) that the missile is capable of carrying over its designated range. Thus, it serves to indicate what size of warhead, or what number of warheads of a certain size, the missile can accommodate. The ICBMs and submarine-launched ballistic missiles (SLBMs) now in service reportedly have throw-weights between about 700 and 7,500 kg.[8]

Aerodynamic or cruise missiles, which are propelled by jet engines, sustain their flight through the use of aerodynamic lift over most of their flight path and travel through the atmosphere parallel to the ground like an aircraft (horizontal trajectory). The most modern cruise missiles can fly below 100 metres from the ground and at a speed of up to 800 kilometres per hour (km/h).[9] They can be guided by remote control or by on-board navigation devices. The latter enable them to dodge obstacles in their path and make their detection by radar more difficult. They have a high level of accuracy.[10]

Airborne nuclear-weapon systems are various types of aircraft that can carry either nuclear bombs or missiles with nuclear warheads. An aircraft carrying gravity ("free fall") bombs may be thought of as a delivery vehicle, while it is more properly denoted a "platform" when carrying missiles.

Delivery vehicles have different ranges. The range is a maximum distance the vehicle can travel from the launching site to the target area. It is determined by the technical capabilities of the delivery vehicle in question. The operational range under particular conditions may be less than this, depending on which military function the weapon system is designated to perform.

C.
Categories of nuclear weapons

Nuclear weapons are assigned different military functions. There is, however, no international consensus on the way of denoting such military assignments or the corresponding weapons. In many cases, these assignments translate into technical requirements of the weapons system, with regard to such characteristics as yield, accuracy, range and means of delivery. For instance, the terms "strategic", "theatre" and "tactical" may have different connotations in different States. Some States do not accept these terms as a means of distinction between different types of nuclear weapons. Indeed, weapons called "tactical" by some might well be used in a way that is, in ordinary language, strategic as seen from the standpoint of the nation against which they are used.[11]

The international literature mostly adheres to the categorization used between the United States and the Soviet Union in the language of certain bilateral treaties in which differentiation between strategic, theatre and tactical missiles and aircraft is made by defining their appropriate ranges. This terminology has been used in the following sections.

Strategic nuclear weapons are generally aimed at an opponent's overall military and economic potential and have long-range or intercontinental capability. Theatre or tactical nuclear weapons may be used against selected military targets on or behind the immediate battlefield (airbases, supply depots, reserve forces) that are related to activities at the battlefield. Consequently, they operate at much shorter ranges than strategic weapons. Weapons envisaged for use against targets in the zone of direct combat are often called battlefield weapons. As a rule they have rather short-range capability or may even be stationary.

1.
Strategic

Strategic nuclear forces consist of land-based intercontinental ballistic missiles (ICBMs), submarine-launched ballistic missiles (SLBMs) and strategic bombers.

Most ICBMs are based in fixed, hardened installations called silos. Others can be rail- or road-mobile. The ICBMs have an intercontinental range of up to 13,000 km. The flight time of an ICBM over its intercontinental range is about 30 minutes. According to official data, presently existing ICBMs carry from one to ten warheads, which may be independently targeted.[12] ICBMs are highly accurate weapons, which is considered to make them suited for attacking hard "point" targets such as an adversary's missile silos.

One of the important characteristics of the SLBM force is that the system as a whole has greater invulnerability as long as the submarines are travelling undetected and are dispersed under the ocean surface. At present, no nation is known to have an anti-submarine capability that threatens this invulnerability. On the other hand, the submarines are widely considered to have a more tenuous communication link with the national command authority, particularly under wartime conditions. The SLBMs have generally been less accurate than land-based missiles and were primarily viewed as weapons to be used against larger and "softer" targets, such as military bases, airfields and possibly population centres. However, the advances in technology increasingly diminish the differences in accuracy between land-based and sea-based ballistic missiles. The SLBMs have a range of up to 12,000 km and may carry up to 14 warheads.[13]

The long-range strategic bombers can be used both for nuclear and non-nuclear missions. In contrast to the ballistic missiles they can also be retargeted *en route* or even recalled. This flexibility is considered a major advantage of the strategic bomber force, while its disadvantages are its vulnerability and low speed, as compared with ICBMs. The strategic bombers combat range can extend up to about 16,000 km and they can carry either gravity bombs or missiles.[14] Air-launched cruise missiles (ALCMs) can be fired from a "stand-off" position, i.e. outside the range of the opponent's air defences. If equipped with effective homing devices, air-launched missiles are considered to be effective against moving targets.

2.
Tactical

This category of nuclear weapons can be deployed on land as well as at sea. The land-based forces include weapons such as ground mobile rockets and missiles, and air-launched bombs and missiles. Yields may vary from 1 kt or less to 1 Mt.

Tactical nuclear weapons deployed at sea are mounted on a variety of ships, submarines, naval aircraft and helicopters, and consist of bombs, surface-to-surface missiles (SSMs), surface-to-air missiles (SAMs) and anti-submarine warfare (ASW) rockets, torpedoes and depth charges.

Some of these systems with very short ranges might be denoted battlefield weapons. For use on a ground battlefield there are short range rockets and artillery shells.

In principle, artillery pieces of about 150 mm calibre or larger are nuclear-capable. Nuclear shells are generally believed to have yields from a fraction of a kiloton up to a few kilotons. The range of nuclear artillery is up to some tens of kilometres.

Atomic demolition munitions (ADMs), which are designed to be used on a battlefield, could create craters and other obstacles to an advancing enemy. These weapons do not appear to be currently deployed by nuclear-weapon States.

D.
Nuclear-weapon arsenals
1.
Strategic arsenals

The composition and development of the strategic nuclear arsenals of the five nuclear-weapon States reflect these countries' military postures, which are by no means identical (see chap. IV). Nevertheless, with the exception of the United Kingdom, the common denominator between them is their reliance on the so-called triad arrangement — land-based, sea-based and bomber forces — but with different emphasis on one or the other leg of the triad. The military rationale for this arrangement lies in the differences of range, yield, accuracy, level of reliability, survivability and readiness between the various types of weapon systems.

A fair amount of information from governmental and academic sources is available on the strategic arsenals of the nuclear-weapon States. As a result of various bilateral disarmament negotiations between the United States and the Soviet Union, much of the official data has been publicly disclosed regarding the overall strength and the general breakdown of strategic forces of these two States.

a.
The United States

The United States considers a triad of nuclear delivery systems a basic prerequisite for the maintenance of its defence posture. Historically, however, the United States first concentrated on manned bombers as its main means of delivery for nuclear weapons. A substantial ICBM and SLBM capacity was developed in the early to mid-1960s.

Concerning the land-based forces, the United States has an estimated 1,000 ICBMs with 2,450 warheads. Some 450 ICBMs are the Minuteman-II, each with a single warhead having a yield of 1-2 Mt. The remaining 500 ICBMs are Minuteman-III with three MIRV warheads, each of either 170 or 335 kt yield. Some of the older Minuteman-III have been replaced by MX missiles. So far, 50 MXs have been deployed in upgraded Minuteman silos. The MX carries 10 MIRV warheads, each of up to about 500 kt, and has a range of over 11,000 km.[15]

As regards the sea-based forces, the United States has 33 sub-marines (SSBNs) equipped with 592 SLBMs and about 5,100 warheads. Some 208 SLBMs are Poseidon missiles with an average of 10 MIRVs, each with a yield of 40 kt. The missile has a range of 4,600 km. The Poseidon missiles were once the mainstay of the United States sea-based nuclear deterrent force, but they are now gradually being replaced by Trident-I (C-4), which has a range of some 7,400 km and is estimated to carry 8 MIRVs of 100 kt each. The United States has already deployed 384 Trident-I SLBMs on Trident SSBNs and on Poseidon SSBNs. The United States also deploys strategic sea-launched cruise missiles (SLCMs). The Tomahawk land-attack mis-sile with a nuclear warhead (TLAM/N) has an estimated range of approximately 2,500 km and has a 5-150 kt warhead. The Tomahawk, in either the strategic/nuclear or tactical/conventional role, is intended to be installed on a large number of naval vessels of all sizes.[16]

The third part of the United States triad consists of approxi-mately 350 strategic bombers with some 4,500 warheads. The bulk of the force consists of B-52s. The other major component comprises some 97 B1-B bombers.

b.
The Soviet Union

The Soviet Union also maintains a triad of nuclear delivery systems, but it has long chosen to emphasize the ICBM arm of its strategic triad. This was due partly to its pioneering ICBM technology and the lack of forward bases for bombers. The SLBMs were develop-ed by the Soviet Union as a complementary, less vulnerable, retalia-tory force against a possible first strike. By the 1970s, the Soviet sea-based nuclear forces had become an effective arm of the nuclear triad.

Currently, the Soviet Union deploys several ICBM systems, totalling 1,356 ICBMs, with approximately 6,450 warheads. Most of the missiles, i.e. some 1,100, were deployed in the period from 1966 to 1979 and consist of SS-11, SS-13, SS-17, SS-18 and SS-19.[17] The last three carry multiple warheads. The SS-18 has a range of about 10,000 km and carries 10 warheads and the SS-19 has a range of 10,000 km with 6 warheads. The yield of both missiles is in the range of several hundred kilotons. The remaining 220 ICBMs are more mod-ern missiles. The SS-24 is a 10-warhead, rail-mobile ICBM and the

SS-25 is a single-warhead, road-mobile ICBM. Both systems have ranges of over 10,000 km.

Concerning the sea-based forces, the Soviet Union has deployed 930 SLBM launchers of various types on SSBs and SSBNs with 3,642 warheads. Out of the total of 62 SSBNs, the Soviet Union maintains 12 Yankee-I class submarines in the Northern and Pacific fleets.[18] They are armed with single warhead missiles.[19] It also deploys the six largest SSBNs currently in service, the 30,000 ton Typhoon-class, each of which is armed with 20 SLBMs (SS-N-20). Only three types of the Soviet SLBMs have MIRVed warheads.[20]

The Soviet Navy also has a sea-launched cruise missile (SS-N-21), comparable to the United States Tomahawk, which it first deployed in 1987. It is presently deployed on submarines.[21]

Regarding bombers, the Soviet Union currently maintains 162 Bear and Blackjack strategic bombers. Some of the bombers are believed to have been recently fitted with cruise missiles. The new Soviet strategic bomber, the Blackjack, has a range similar to that of the United States B1-B bomber.[22]

c.

The United Kingdom

The United Kingdom has never simultaneously deployed a nuclear triad, although at different times it has had in service bombers, land-based and sea-based ballistic missiles.

During the 1950s, the United Kingdom concentrated mostly on its bomber force. By 1963, it also operated 60 United States Thor land-based missiles, which gave the British the combined capability of reaching as many as 230 possible targets.[23] At this time, the United Kingdom had two legs of a triad: land-based medium-range missiles and bombers.

In 1963, the United Kingdom acquired the technology from the United States to build 4 Polaris SSBNs, each equipped with 16 single warhead SLBMs.[24] By 1970, it had abandoned the other two legs of the triad and since then has maintained a "one-dimensional" strategic force.

At present, these 4 British Polaris SSBNs are each equipped with 16 missiles, carrying two warheads (MRV). Thus, the United Kingdom has in its strategic force a total of 64 SLBMs with 128 warheads.[25]

d.

France

France maintains a nuclear triad composed of bombers, land-based intermediate/medium-range ballistic missiles (IRBMs) and SLBMs. The French "force de dissuasion" (deterrent) is considerably smaller than that of either the United States or the Soviet Union.

The French nuclear bomber force consists of 20 Mirage IV with a combat radius of some 1,500 km each with a payload of two 70 kt bombs or one 300 kt bomb. In recent years, some of these bombers have also been equipped with the ASMP short-range attack missile with a range of 100-300 km to give them a "stand-off" capability.[26] These missiles are intended to improve the survivability and penetration ability of the aircraft's nuclear weapons.

As regards the ballistic missiles, France deploys 18 IRBMs (S-3), each with one 1 Mt warhead. These have a range of 3,500 km.

The most important part of the French triad is its SLBMs, which presently consist of 6 SSBNs with a total of 256 warheads. Four of them are equipped with 16 SLBMs (M-20) each, which carry a single 1 Mt warhead and have a range of 3,000 km. Two submarines have been retrofitted with new SLBMs (M-4) with 6 MIRVed warheads and a range of 4,000-5,000 km.

e.

China

China has also adopted the triad approach to its nuclear force posture. Its strategic forces are the smallest of the five nuclear-weapon States.

The oldest leg of its triad are the bombers. China deploys two types of manned bombers: the IL-28 and the TU-16. Their total number is believed to be between 120 and 150 aircraft, with a range of up to 1,850 km and 5,900 km, respectively. The IL-28 is capable of carrying one 20 kt-3 Mt bomb, and the TU-16 three 20 kt-3 Mt bombs.

The Chinese ground-based missile force consists of approximately 150 missiles, none of which have multiple warheads. Some of them are ICBMs with a range of 13,000 km.

With a successful test in September 1988, China has also developed an SLBM capability. It now deploys 2 submarines with 12 SLBMs (CSS-N-3) on them. The missile has a range of 3,300 km and carries one warhead with a yield of between 200 kt and 1 Mt.

2.
Tactical and battlefield arsenals

a.
Land-based

Following the 1987 INF Treaty between the United States and the Soviet Union, which provides for the elimination of land-based ballistic and cruise missiles of intermediate and shorter-range (5,000-500 km), only missiles of ranges less than 500 km remain in the tactical arsenals of these two nuclear-weapon States (see chap. VIII). NATO countries (other than France) deploy 88 Lance missile launchers with warheads in the low-kiloton range in Europe. The Soviet Union deploys in Europe 1,608 short-range missile launchers,[27] some of which have warheads in the high-kiloton range.

The nuclear warheads assigned to tactical and battlefield missions are kept in special storage sites on the territories of some of the United States allies in Europe and Asia. An academic source estimated the total number of United States nuclear warheads abroad assigned to land-based systems to be in the range of some 6,500 in 1985. Although the great majority of these were based in the Federal Republic of Germany and in the United Kingdom, smaller numbers were deployed in Italy, Turkey, Greece, South Korea, the Netherlands and Belgium.[28] Following the reduction or replacement of part of the European stock of warheads[29] (pursuant to earlier NATO decisions), another unofficial source[30] put the number of United States tactical and battlefield warheads stored in Europe in 1988 in the range of 4,600.

Academic sources[31] indicate that the Soviet Union keeps tactical nuclear weapons in the German Democratic Republic, Poland, Czechoslovakia and Hungary, presumably involving a "double-key" system of control and Soviet custodianship. As at 1989, over 1,000 Soviet tactical aircraft were forward-based at military facilities in the four countries.[32] According to the Soviet Union, with the current withdrawal of its troops from Hungary and Czechoslovakia, Soviet nuclear weapons outside its territory will remain only in the German Democratic Republic and Poland until arrangements on tactical nuclear weapons in Europe make their presence there unnecessary.

Some of the United Kingdom's tactical and battlefield land-based nuclear weapons are deployed in the Federal Republic of Germany.

France has a short-range tactical nuclear force equipped with 44 Pluton ballistic missiles presumably with a 25 kt warhead and a range of about 120 km. France considers these to be pre-strategic rather than tactical weapons.

As regards land-based nuclear-capable aircraft, the United States forces in Europe deploy 65 medium-range bombers (FB-111A) and 300-400 forward-based strike aircraft (F-4, F-111 and others). The Soviet Union deploys 330 medium-range bombers (TU-22 Blinder and TU-22M Backfire), and also a large number of short-range strike aircraft.

Both the United States and the Soviet Union have developed artillery shells in the calibre range 152-240 mm and have deployed several hundreds of them in Europe. They are generally believed to have yields from a fraction of a kiloton up to a few kilotons.[33]

Although the United States is known to have produced atomic demolition munitions (ADMs), no peacetime emplacement of ADMs is believed to have taken place. Furthermore, all of the existing munitions of this nature are to be completely withdrawn from the United States armed forces.[34]

b.
Sea-based

The United States and the Soviet Union have substantial numbers of tactical nuclear weapons deployed at sea.

The main tactical nuclear system of the United States is its several hundred aircraft stationed on 14 carriers, which form the core of the major naval task forces. Their range is between 550 and 1,800 km. Each aircraft can carry one or two bombs with yields that reportedly vary from 20 kt to 1 Mt.

For the purpose of anti-submarine warfare (ASW), the United States had deployed on most of the major classes of its surface vessels a number of nuclear-capable missiles with various ranges. While more detailed figures on these missiles are not available, in early 1989 reports were published to the effect that the United States Navy had decided to retire these nuclear systems, while retaining the option to introduce a new system. This retirement now seems to have taken place.

The United States Navy has nuclear-capable ASW aircraft and helicopters. The ASW aircraft may have a range of up to 3,800 km, and can carry one depth bomb, presumably of up to 20 kt yield. Their total number is not known.

The Soviet Union also deploys tactical nuclear weapons on board its fleet of vertical/short take-off and landing (V/STOL) aircraft-carriers and guided-missile cruisers.[35]

Other Soviet surface vessels such as cruisers, destroyers and small craft are also equipped with a variety of surface-to-surface missiles (SSMs). Their range is estimated to be from 60 to 550 km and their warhead yields are in the medium kiloton range.

For the purpose of ASW, the Soviet Navy deploys several hundred ASW aircraft, each of which can carry one nuclear depth bomb. In addition to these aircraft, the Soviet Union also deploys several hundred ASW nuclear-tipped missiles.

E.
Systems for command and control of nuclear forces

1.
General

To ensure that the political and military leaders of the nuclear-weapon States have access to relevant and timely information and that they remain in communication with their nuclear forces and each other, it is necessary to have an elaborate system of reconnaissance, data-processing facilities and communication networks. The two major Powers in particular have paid great attention to such systems. Some of their components are space-based sensors or communication links, others are ground-based and still others could be airborne. The totality of these assets, with their associated procedures and routines, is often referred to as "C^3I", which stands for command, control, communications and intelligence. In some cases, C^3I facilities have been hardened against nuclear attack to permit them to operate in a post-attack environment.[36]

The sensors include early warning satellites intended to detect missile launches and big ground-based radar stations to follow the trajectories of the missiles. The communication links include relay satellites and ground-based radio links. Most of the command centres are located in well protected underground shelters, but there are also some airborne emergency command posts.[37]

2.

Release procedure

As regards the United States, the President retains full authority over the use of nuclear weapons. If the President should become incapacitated, the Vice-President would assume responsibility.

The United States nuclear forces have an array of safeguards established to minimize the risk of unauthorized use. For tactical weapons a system called permissive action links (PALs) was established in the early 1960s.[38] They use some kind of electronic locking system that guards against unauthorized use of the weapons. Some of these systems have the ability to disable or destroy a nuclear weapon in response to certain types of tampering. The control systems guard only the warhead, not the launch system. They exist both on weapons in the United States and on United States warheads attached to NATO commands in Europe.

The United States Strategic Air Command has an additional mechanism, a bomber coded switch system, which requires a correct code to open the aircraft's bomb bay doors.[39]

The United States ICBMs require two men to complete the procedure to launch. Since 1985, the command and control system for these missiles has become more robust. Every 10 missiles are controlled by a launch control centre (LCC), which passes on the unlock code. Until 1985, missile crews had physical control of the unlock codes, although they still operated under the "two-man" system. Now, all unlock codes are passed down from higher authorities.[40]

The procedure on United States ships, particularly SSBNs, is somewhat different. There is no PAL system. However, a large number of officers must be involved in the firing process, once authorized. In the case of SSBNs, a firing message is received and confirmed by two separate teams of men. Special keys are issued to responsible crew members and a series of "permission" switches must be engaged in the correct order to fire a weapon. The entire crew is informed of each step of the procedure.[41]

As in the United States, the exclusive responsibility for the use of all Soviet nuclear weapons is entrusted to the President of the Soviet Union as the Commander-in-Chief of the Soviet armed forces. In the event of the incapacitation of the Soviet President, his powers are transferred to the Chairman of the Supreme Soviet.

The decision for launch would be handed down from the President to the General Staff of the military. They would then communicate either to the Strategic Rocket Forces or directly to individual command posts. The only part of the Soviet military that is on a day-to-day alert are the strategic rocket forces and reportedly around 10 per cent of the SSBN force. Soviet ICBMs use a multiple-key system, similar to the one in use in the United States.

As is the case with United States nuclear forces in Europe, the Soviet Union retains sole control over its nuclear warheads assigned to the defence of Warsaw Treaty countries, whether those weapons are stationed in its own territory or on the territory of its allies.

The British nuclear command and control system in many ways parallels the procedure used in the United States. Only the Prime Minister can order the launch of the British nuclear weapons. Submarine captains also seem to have firing authority if the North Atlantic Council is silent for a predetermined period of time. The individual submarines have positive controls similar to American submarines, a two-man key system. Like the United States, the United Kingdom has no PALs on its SSBNs; rather, the message is read to the crew and two separate teams of officers confirm it. Keys are then issued by pre-launch officers to launching officers while all actions are read to the crew. The keys switch on "permission" links for launching.[42]

As regards French nuclear forces, all control for launching resides with the President of the Republic. The Prime Minister is next in line of succession. Like the United Kingdom and United States, the French have a two-man system for nuclear weapons use, i.e. two individuals must receive two separate codes and engage them simultaneously.[43]

Information on the Chinese C^3I system is almost non-existent. To keep in touch with its SSBNs, China uses very low frequency (VLF) for world-wide communications, like other navies. No information is available on the Chinese ICBMs' command and control. It would seem reasonable that China has some kind of a PAL system for its nuclear systems. It is also presumed that the Chinese Government exercises as strict control over its military command system as is the case with other nuclear-weapon States.

3.

Handling of nuclear weapons

With a view to minimizing the risk of nuclear weapons accidents, false alarms, unauthorized launches, terrorist attacks, theft, sabotage or seizure in countries where nuclear weapons are deployed, the nuclear-weapon States have developed various safety measures for storing and handling of nuclear weapons.

There are a variety of technical devices on United States nuclear weapons to protect against unauthorized use, tampering and accidents (PALs, safing wires, insensitive high explosives, etc.); such devices are estimated to make the chance of an accidental nuclear explosion negligible.[44] These precautions are also taken with United States nuclear weapons located in Europe. Nuclear weapons are stored in special "igloos", which have special protective measures, including automatic immobilization devices for intruders.[45]

The United States supplies almost all of the nuclear warheads assigned to NATO's defence. The custodial teams for the weapons are drawn from the United States military, who would release the weapons to authorized units, after authorization for use was received. The United States controls internal security while the host nation controls site and transportation security.[46] These United States custodial teams have the responsibility for control over United States nuclear weapons stored in host nations.

There are a number of controls on nuclear weapons at all nuclear storage sites, which are heavily guarded and hardened. Further, there are double barbed-wire fences with double locks and these are unlocked by two different people.[47] There are many storage igloos at each site, some of which may possibly be decoys.[48] Individual American soldiers who handle nuclear weapons have to complete the Personnel Reliability Programme and are broken up into two different types of access: "critical", which gives access to nuclear weapons for quality control, maintenance and inspections; and "controlled", which gives access to those with non-technical knowledge, or those involved in handling and assembly positions. Together, these two positions make up the two-man system and only United States citizens who have passed a rigorous security screening can occupy a "critical" position.[49]

British procedures for handling and storing nuclear weapons are similar to those of the United States. The United Kingdom maintains sovereignty over its nuclear weapons, but there is a high degree of cooperation with the United States in these matters.

Since the beginning of its military nuclear programme, France has devoted particular attention to nuclear safety and security. Since 1960, it has developed concepts, procedures and instruments to improve such safety and security. While the details of these operations are classified, according to French authorities they have produced satisfactory results.

According to Soviet sources, in the Soviet Union nuclear weapons are handled only by specially selected and trained officers and warrant officers. Each of them has to pass a yearly screening for reliability and competence by a commission of experts, including physicians and psychologists. On the average, from 4 to 6 per cent of those screened do not pass the tests and are not reconfirmed for the job.[50] Furthermore, according to these sources, the Soviet Union has also introduced PALs and multiple-key systems and keeps its nuclear weapons stored in heavily fortified depots guarded by specially trained military units. Those depots are equipped with safety and warning systems reinforcing each other to prevent an unauthorized person or a group of persons from getting hold of nuclear weapons. The weapons would also automatically become inoperable if tampered with by unauthorized persons.

Notes

1. Unless otherwise indicated, numerical data in this chapter are based on Stockholm International Peace Research Institute, *SIPRI Yearbook 1990: World Armaments and Disarmament*, Oxford, Oxford University Press, 1990, pp. 3-50.

2. *Comprehensive Study on Nuclear Weapons* (United Nations publication, Sales No. E.81.I.11), para. 9.

3. The warhead that exploded over Hiroshima had a yield of approximately 13 kt and the one exploded over Nagasaki had a yield of 22 kt. Thomas B. Cochran, William A. Arkin and Milton M. Hoenig, *Nuclear Weapons Databook: Vol. 1, United States Nuclear Forces*, Cambridge, Ballinger, 1984, p. 32.

4. This mass can range from 15-25 kg for uranium-235 and from 4-8 kg for plutonium-239.

5. *Comprehensive Study on Nuclear Weapons* (United Nations publication, Sales No. E.81.I.11), paras. 12 and 17.

6. This so-called enrichment can be carried on to attain different concentrations of U-235 in the final product. Uranium with 3-4 per cent U-235 can fuel a commercial light water reactor. Some other types of reactors use more highly enriched uranium with 20-90 per cent U-235. The term "weapon-grade" usually denotes a U-235 content over 90 per cent. The process of atomic vapour laser isotope separation has also been examined as a possibility to eventually augment or replace the gaseous diffusion plants. Once installed, it was found to

cost less per separative work unit (kg SWU) and require less energy than other enrichment techniques.

7.   Cochran *et al.*, *op. cit.*, pp. 23 and 24.
8.   Bernard Blake, ed., *Jane's Weapons Systems 1988-1989*, Surrey, Jane's Information Group Ltd., 1988, pp. 1-34.
9.   *Ibid.*, p. 460.
10.   See *Cruise Missiles: Background, Technology and Verification*, Ottawa, Department of External Affairs, 1987, pp. 22-26.
11.   See Lawrence Freedman, *The Evolution of Nuclear Strategy*, New York, St. Martin's Press, 1981, p. 118.
12.   Frank Carlucci, *US Secretary of Defense Annual Report to the Congress, Fiscal Year 1990*, Washington, US Government Printing Office, 1989, p. 187.
13.   *IISS Military Balance 1989-90*, IISS, 1989, p. 212. *Jane's Weapons Systems, 1988-1989*, p. 30 for range and CEP of D-5 SLBM.
14.   *Jane's All the World's Aircraft 1988-1989*, Surrey, Jane's Information Group Ltd., 1988, pp. 368 and 369. See also *Soviet Military Power*, Washington, US Government Printing Office, 1989, p. 45.
15.   *SIPRI Yearbook 1990* gives the yield 300 kt for the MX warhead (para. 336).
16.   *Jane's Weapons Systems 1988-1989*, pp. 459 and 460, provides detailed information on the vessels involved.
17.   Designators for Soviet weapons used throughout the study are largely those available in Western sources, as Soviet designators have not been generally published. The correspondence between Soviet and NATO designators for Soviet missiles specified in the SALT II treaty is as follows: RS-16 = SS-17; RS-18 = SS-19; RS-20 = SS-18; RSM-50 = SS-N-18.
18.   Regarding stationing, see *SIPRI Yearbook 1989*, p. 14; also *Soviet Military Power 1989*, p. 48. Since 1980, of a total of 29, the Soviet Union has retired some 17 Yankee-I class SSBNs in accordance with the limits set out in the 1979 SALT II Agreement.
19.   Except the SS-N-6, which carries 2 MIRVed warheads. See *SIPRI Yearbook 1990*, p. 16.
20.   *Jane's Weapons Systems 1988-1989*, p. 907. For the SS-N-8, see also *SIPRI Yearbook 1990*, p. 16.
21.   See *IISS Military Balance 1989-90*, pp. 6 and 30. For SS-N-21, see also *Soviet Military Power 1989*, pp. 47 and 76.
22.   *Jane's All the World's Aircraft 1988-1989*, p. 269.
23.   Lawrence Freedman, "British nuclear targeting", in Desmond Ball and Jeffrey Richelson, eds, *Strategic Nuclear Targeting*, Ithaca, New York and London, Cornell University Press, 1986.
24.   *Jane's Weapons Systems 1988-1989*, p. 907.
25.   *SIPRI Yearbook 1990*, p. 20, states that only 96 warheads are actually deployed.
26.   See François Heisbourg, "British and French nuclear forces" in *Survival*, July-August 1989, p. 309. See also "Loi de programmation militaire", in *Armée d'Aujourd'hui*, No. 120, 1987, p. 45.
27.   They are referred to as Frog 7, Scud-B and SS-21. For stationing, see *SIPRI Yearbook 1989*, p. 22.
28.   William M. Arkin and Richard W. Fieldhouse, *Nuclear Battlefields. Global Links in the Arms Race*, Cambridge, Mass., Ballinger, 1985, p. 147; see also

Simon Duke, *United States Military Forces and Installations in Europe*, Oxford, Oxford University Press, 1989, p.172.

29. Duke, *op cit.*, p. 172.

30. Robert E. Harkavy, *Bases Abroad: The Global Foreign Military Presence*, SIPRI, Oxford University Press, 1989, pp. 262 and 263.

31. *Ibid.*

32. *SIPRI Yearbook 1989*, pp. 16-23.

33. Harkavy, *op. cit.*, p. 263.

34. However, in Carlucci, *op. cit.*, p. 151, the talk is of upgrading these systems, not retiring them.

35. *SIPRI Yearbook 1989*, p. 24.

36. Ashton B. Carter *et al.*, *Managing Nuclear Operations*, Washington, Brookings Institution, 1987, pp. 546 and 547.

37. *Ibid.*, p. 97.

38. There are four types of PALS, designated A, B, D and F. See also Harkavy, *op. cit.*, p. 262.

39. Donald Cotter, "Peacetime operations, safety and security" in Carter, *op. cit.*, p. 50.

40. *Ibid.*, pp. 50 and 51.

41. *Ibid.*, p. 52.

42. Catherine McArdle Kelleher, "NATO nuclear operations", in Carter, *op. cit.*, p. 466.

43. *Ibid.*, p. 468.

44. Cotter, *op. cit.*, pp. 43-45.

45. *Ibid.*, pp. 52 and 53.

46. Kelleher, *op. cit.*, p. 452 and 453.

47. *Ibid.*, p. 456.

48. *Ibid.*, p. 455.

49. Cotter, *op. cit.*, pp. 60 and 61.

50. *Arguments and Facts*, Moscow, No. 18, 1990.

III
Trends in the technological development of nuclear-weapon systems

A.
General

Nuclear weapons have undergone tremendous change and development since their inception some 45 years ago. Apart from the basic principle of nuclear reactions as the source of energy, there remains very little resemblance between the first two bombs exploded at Hiroshima and Nagasaki, which were technically very primitive, and the ballistic missiles equipped with a number of multiple independently targetable re-entry vehicles (MIRVs) in the nuclear weapon arsenals today.

While there is no doubt that this sophistication of nuclear weapons has been made possible by the application of modern science and technology, the role of science and technology in nuclear-weapon developments has been interpreted in different ways. Thus, there are those who see the ongoing technological development of nuclear weapons as being necessitated by threats to national security and as a corollary to the evolution of theories or doctrines regarding the possible use of nuclear weapons. Newer nuclear-weapon systems usually incorporate improved command and control features and improved resistance to accidental detonation. There are also those, however, who believe that new weapon systems have sometimes emerged not because of any particular military or security consideration, but rather because technology (in conjunction with bureaucratic and other forces) may take the lead, creating weapons for which needs have to be invented and deployment theories have to be readjusted. In this connection, concern has been expressed about the extent to which scientific and technical manpower is engaged in military research and development and that such involvement leads to the production of new and more sophisticated weapons.[1]

An action-reaction phenomenon in arms competition among States cannot be excluded either as one influential aspect in the ongoing development of nuclear weapons. Many believe that this phenomenon reflects the interplay of expectations between the States, which results in similar systems being copied and defensive and offensive systems being designed in the expectation of new challenges from other States. In their view, the problem is exacerbated by the secrecy that surrounds the weapons research and development process in many countries, which leads to worst-case assumptions on the part of other States of the putative threat that such developments may pose. They are also concerned that the military research and development effort's own momentum and the resulting new weapons options could thus contribute to an open-ended arms competition.

B.
Main features of past developments

1.
Nuclear warheads

The first turning point in the development of warheads was the successful utilization, in the early 1950s, of fusion reactions in nuclear explosives. This made it possible to produce thermonuclear devices capable of releasing extremely large amounts of energy.[2]

As a result, through the 1950s and early 1960s, the tendency was generally to build more powerful weapons, i.e. with a greater explosive yield.[3] The fact that throughout most of the period a bomber force was the main means of delivery was an important consideration as well. This trend was also in line with the prevailing doctrinal concept at that time of the use of nuclear weapons against population centres (see chap. IV).

On the other hand, a development to reduce the size and weight of warheads was also initiated in the 1950s. As a consequence, it became technically feasible to produce various small nuclear charges for a variety of non-strategic uses, thus considerably expanding the potential role of nuclear weapons in a conflict situation. For instance, nuclear artillery shells were first tested in 1953.[4]

The technical development of nuclear warheads entailed not only reductions in their size and weight in absolute terms. It was also possible to increase their yield-to-weight ratio, particularly by the use of fusion devices. One result of this was that it became possible to put multiple warheads on strategic missiles (see chap. II).

For strategic warheads, the trend towards larger yields was reversed during the 1970s, especially in the United States. The fact that warheads with considerably lower yields were introduced was related mainly to significant improvements in the accuracy of the delivery systems, in particular ICBMs. The higher accuracy entails a much higher ratio between the lethality and the yield of a nuclear warhead, when employed against a small ("point") target.

In addition to these major developments regarding nuclear warheads, several other less known but related technological improvements were also pursued. They concerned warhead safety, reliability, versatility and hardening against adverse environments. Safety measures were aimed at minimizing both the risk of accidents in handling the weapons and the possibility of unauthorized use. For this purpose insensitive high explosives were introduced, as well as a multitude of arming and safing devices, including the PALs. Reliability of warheads was enhanced in several ways, such as by developing special materials to prevent deterioration of weapon components or special designs to withstand the tremendous acceleration in a gun tube. Versatility was enhanced by designing a warhead in such a way that different yields could be selected easily.

During the 40-year period from 1945 to 1985 about 100 accidents have been reported that damaged and might conceivably have caused unintended detonation of a nuclear weapon.[5] These accidents include airplane crashes, unintended dropping of nuclear weapons from airplanes, explosions in ammunition depots or fires on board submarines. So far, however, none of those accidents has led to the unintended detonation of a nuclear weapon.

One way of pursuing versatility, through diversification of the nuclear inventory, is the "tailoring" of warheads to enhance or suppress various effects of the explosion. This is done by selecting different fission-to-fusion ratios to produce the desired total yield, combined with different designs of the casing and other structural components of the warhead.[6]

The best-known example of "tailoring" is the "enhanced radiation" weapon or the so-called "neutron bomb", a weak fusion device with a special design. Basically, it could produce much higher levels of initial neutron radiation than an ordinary fission weapon of equal yield, while at the same time suppressing the level of blast and heat, thus considerably reducing the expected damage to the surroundings. The United States developed and tested a neutron warhead but did not put it on the production line. The Soviet Union limited its efforts to a research programme. Regarding France, it has indicated that the actual state of research would allow it, if necessary, to produce a neutron weapon.[7]

It appears that some other technological developments related to the warhead that had been pursued by nuclear-weapon States were ultimately suspended or abandoned. For instance, it is technically possible to produce warheads with very low explosive yields (by deliberately not making full use of the fissile material). However, there were concerns that a wide deployment of such warheads, the so-called "mini-nukes", with their limited radius of material damage, would possibly lead to a "conventionalization" of their use. After some international debate, the United States, the United Kingdom and the Soviet Union declared that they would not for the time being deploy nuclear weapons with small yields in such a way as to blur the nuclear threshold.[8]

The 1980 United Nations study on nuclear weapons noted in connection with nuclear warhead developments that the reduction of their physical size was, in some applications, close to the limits set by the laws of physics, and that despite the research and development in the field of special types of warheads, no major breakthrough was likely to occur with regard to the basic design principles of nuclear explosives. It concluded that the evolution of delivery systems seemed likely to carry more practical importance in the future, as it had already done for some time.[9] This conclusion still seems valid.

2.
Delivery systems

The only nuclear warheads ever used in an armed conflict were delivered to their targets — Hiroshima and Nagasaki — in 1945 by ordinary bomber aircraft. Other forms of delivery vehicles for nuclear warheads were developed later. For instance, ground-launched ballistic missiles were first introduced in the 1950s and submarine-launched ballistic missiles around 1960. The first cruise missiles (CM) with nuclear warheads were developed in the 1950s, while longer-range CMs with sophisticated navigation aids became available much later — in the late 1970s.[10]

The early versions of ballistic missiles were fairly inaccurate and were thus considered to be unable to hit any targets smaller than cities or large installations (industrial, commercial or military). If the missile was intended to destroy a point target, such as one of the adversary's missile launchers, a high weapon yield would be needed to compensate for the possible deviation of the warhead from its calculated trajectory.

Missile accuracy is usually given in terms of the circular error probable (CEP), defined as the distance from an aiming point within which, on the average, half the shots aimed at this point will fall. Using this concept, assessments of the efficiency of various missile systems can be illustrated. For example, a 1 Mt nuclear warhead may be needed in order to destroy a particular hardened structure if the CEP of that nuclear weapon is 1 km. The same effect could result from a 125 kt warhead with a 0.5 km CEP accuracy, or a 40 kt warhead with 0.33 km CEP. Thus, increased accuracy meant that smaller yield warheads could replace high yield warheads as a threat to these types of targets.[11]

In other words, the nominal yield could be decreased while the effective lethality of the weapons increased. This had rather profound military effects, as it made it increasingly more difficult to protect land-based missiles from an attack, i.e. a first-strike aimed at eliminating these weapons. This required increased "hardening" of the missile silos since the existing ones no longer provided sufficient protection. This consideration, in part, bolstered further development of SLBMs, which were generally considered far less vulnerable than any other type of nuclear weapons, and more recently also led to the development of mobile ICBMs. It also prompted quantitative increases of the strategic inventories.

It was argued by strategists that if ICBMs were left vulnerable to first-strike attacks, this could conceivably force the respective country to prepare for a possible use-them-or-lose-them scenario. Conversely, measures to decrease their vulnerability would support the deterrent posture of the respective country by enhancing its "second strike" capability. One such measure is the development of mobile ballistic missiles.

At the time of the preparation of the 1980 United Nations study on nuclear weapons, definite CEP values for different existing nuclear-weapon systems were not available, for reasons both of military secrecy and, presumably, insufficient basic knowledge. Also CEP values varied considerably depending on the system in question. Some of the academic sources at the time had given estimates for both United States and Soviet ICBMs as approaching a CEP of about 200 metres. Other weapon systems were generally considered less accurate, an aspect that was given a great deal of attention in subsequent years. Accuracy has improved considerably since then.

Another development in delivery systems was the introduction of multiple warheads on missiles. The first generation of multi-warhead systems became known as "multiple re-entry vehicles" (MRV). The missile carries several warheads (2-4), thus considerably increasing the probability of the target's destruction. The next generation, called "multiple independently targeted re-entry vehicles" (MIRV), is capable of directing each warhead against different individual targets located at varying distances up to perhaps 500 km from each other. This development has increased the effectiveness of ballistic missiles.[12]

The MRV warheads were deployed in the United States towards the mid-1960s on SLBMs, and MIRVs around 1970 on both ICBMs and SLBMs. By the 1980s, both the United States and the Soviet Union had deployed either MRVs or MIRVs on their major weapon systems.[13] The other three nuclear-weapon States had also been developing similar technologies, which some of them deployed in subsequent years.

As early as around 1970, there was some discussion regarding the development of a third generation of multiple warheads, the so-called "maneouverable re-entry vehicle" (MARV) technology. The main characteristic of these warheads would be their ability to readjust their flight patterns after having re-entered the atmosphere. The main purpose of this would be to increase their probability of penetrating an ABM defence. With the aid of autonomous sensors, the MARV might also be able to attack mobile targets with a higher degree of accuracy.

The American and Soviet cruise missiles deployed during the 1960s (on aircraft and, by the Soviet Union, on ships) had comparatively short ranges, up to about 600 km.[14] They were believed to be intended for use mainly against surface ships.

By the 1980s, the development of modern cruise missiles had gained momentum, owing to advances in propulsion and navigation technology, even though problems remained. With ranges up to at least 2,500 km and an expected accuracy of a few tens of metres, cruise missiles were envisaged to fill both a strategic role — in their air-launched version (ALCM) — and theatre roles when deployed on ships (SLCM) or on ground-mobile launchers (GLCM).[15]

There was also ongoing development as regards platforms for the launching of various types of missiles. By 1980, further hardening of ICBM silos was not deemed appropriate. For this reason, a great deal of attention was devoted to various schemes for ground-mobile ICBM launchers. The Soviet Union had already deployed its SS-20 medium-range ballistic missile in a mobile mode.[16]

The main features in the development of strategic submarines, aside from improvements of their missiles, were related to increased radius of action and more silent propulsion. More advanced navigational aids allowed increased precision in fixing the position of a submarine and hence increased accuracy of SLBMs.

Aircraft were modernized and modified to accommodate new types of nuclear weapons (ALCMs) or larger numbers of weapons, but no aircraft seemed to have been designed to serve solely as a nuclear-weapon platform.

3.
Other components

The other components of modern nuclear-weapon systems were also subject to various technological developments in the field. Guidance systems and some components of C^3I systems were of particular interest, even though they are too complex to be explored here in all their possible combinations.

Guidance systems for missiles, and for some types of mobile platforms, utilize many different techniques.[17] To improve long-range navigation, the inertial guidance system that had long been used needed to be supplemented by intermittent, precise position information provided, for instance, by a set of satellites in geostationary orbit.

For homing a weapon on the target, a number of techniques are being developed, primarily for use in the conventional arms field. The essential part of these homing systems are sensors, which include a variety of radar, infra-red and laser devices.[18] It was believed that some of them were possible to use within strategic vehicles and others to enhance the accuracy of various tactical nuclear weapons. Any actual deployment of these technological developments was not, however, thought to have taken place before 1980.

Improvements in C^3I technology — which exploit the rapid advances in electronics and information and data processing — aim at increasing the reliability, survivability and speed of the systems. By 1980 additional impetus had been given to this work by some recently detected flaws in the United States C^3I system.[19] A reliable communications system is also crucial to nuclear-war fighting.[20]

C.
Main features of new developments

Unlike in the 1950s, 1960s and early 1970s, when major technological breakthroughs occurred in a number of important areas and took place at an accelerated speed, the technological development of nuclear-weapon systems in the 1980s has been in general less dramatic and largely focused on several specific areas as a follow-up to previous developments. Changes in emphasis on nuclear-war fighting and space-based defensive systems have also been noted.

In the area of nuclear warheads, technology has advanced incrementally to make warheads safer, more reliable and more flexible, i.e. capable of variable yields, possibly also requiring less fissile material to produce a given yield.

Apart from this, efforts are reportedly being made to improve warhead technology in several specific ways. One concerns the continued development of an earth-penetrating warhead, which could burrow deep into the ground before exploding. It would be used to hold underground targets, primarily command and control centres, at risk. Because this would place command and control itself at risk, it could be viewed as a serious development with potentially destabilizing consequences. Another effort is related to the MARV concept described above.

However, despite the enhanced capability that both penetration and MARVed warheads may offer, reportedly neither technology has been deployed so far on a weapon system.

Reportedly, the trend towards greater accuracy of ballistic missiles continues. During the 1980s, this does not seem to have been accompanied by continued lower yields of strategic warheads, however. For instance, the MX ICBM is described as carrying warheads with selectable yields of 300 or 475 kt each, as opposed to the 170 kt warheads on Minuteman-III missiles deployed in the 1970s.[21]

In the area of delivery vehicles, several new developments have taken place. Concerning land-based missile forces, two features are of particular military significance: the more widespread replacement of liquid fuel rockets with solid fuel and the introduction of mobile ICBMs.

Apart from considerably diminishing the safety risks involved in handling liquid fuel, the most important aspect of the use of solid fuel is that it significantly reduces the time necessary to prepare missiles for launch, thus enhancing military preparedness of nuclear forces. Solid fuel technology was introduced in the United States in the 1960s and in the French missile forces beginning in the early 1980s. It is a more recent development in the Soviet Union where it has been implemented only for the most modern missile systems. China still uses liquid fuel for its missiles.[22]

Development of mobile missiles has continued and also covers the strategic area. There are currently two mobile ICBMs, the Soviet SS-24 and SS-25. Both missiles are solid-fueled.[23] In the United States, a discussion has been under way on the possibility of developing a new single-warhead road-mobile ICBM (Midgetman), or deploying the existing MX ICBMs on railroad cars. Neither plan has yet been formally endorsed by the United States Government.

The major developments concerning the strategic air forces of nuclear-weapon States have been the advent of stealth technology for advanced bombers and air-launched cruise missiles.

Stealth technology is a combination of aircraft design, improved electronics and special material coatings designed to absorb radar waves. This technology is intended to enable aircraft and missiles to fly undetected by existing radar systems in carrying out their mission.

Countermeasures to stealth technology are being explored, which include various special forms of radar, such as very low-frequency, bistatic or carrier-free radar. None of these techniques is yet capable of negating stealth technology, however.[24]

In the United States, the B-2, or Stealth Bomber, is the most advanced aircraft to employ stealth technology.[25] It can carry both conventional and nuclear weapons. Among the B-2 missions is destruction of mobile nuclear missiles and hardened command centres. The bomber has been developed and flight-tested, but not yet deployed.

The United States B-1B bomber is also a new development, in that it is a dual-capable, long-range strategic bomber capable of conforming to a multitude of roles ranging from deep-strike solo penetration of enemy territory to maritime surveillance and aerial mine-laying. These varied roles have not previously been combined into the capability of a single aircraft. Some 97 B-1B bombers have been deployed during the 1980s.[26]

The Soviet Union has developed the Blackjack (TU-160), a supersonic bomber for penetration missions. It also has the capability for stand-off missions, and may also possess a maritime role. The deployment of this aircraft began in the late 1980s. By the end of 1989, 17 aircraft of this type had been deployed.[27]

Air-launched cruise missiles (ALCMs) are designed to allow manned bombers to avoid having to face the challenge of heavy air defences while performing their mission, as they are able to launch their ALCMs before penetrating enemy air space. Thus, ALCMs effectively replace the gravity bomb and give older bombers, such as the American B-52 or the Soviet Bear, increased longevity. The sophisticated guidance system employed on ALCMs also increases the accuracy of bomber-delivered weapons.

Research is also under way for advanced cruise missiles (ACM) that would use stealth technology, as well as for an advanced strategic air-launched missile that would achieve supersonic speeds. Both these types of missiles would be providing maximum penetration ability against air defences. Two new cruise missiles under development in the Soviet Union reportedly employ stealth technology, the short-range attack missile (SRAM) AS-16 and the supersonic AS-X-19 ALCM.[28] France is also developing a miniaturized independently targetable warhead, the TN-75, to be carried on a modified M-4 ballistic missile that may incorporate stealth technology.[29]

In the area of maritime nuclear forces, apart from continuing efforts to make nuclear submarines ever more quiet and to improve communication links with them, the two main development features of the 1980s have been the continued replacement of single-warhead and MRV missiles with MIRVed missiles, on the one hand, and the development and deployment of sea-launched cruise missiles

(SLCM), on the other. There has also been a corresponding improvement in the CEP, both of the MIRVs and SLCMs.

Both the United States and the Soviet Union are thought to be improving their SLBM forces with regard to accuracy. Analysts have suggested that the United States Trident-II (D-5) will have a CEP of about 120 metres, similar to that of the Minuteman-II ICBM. The new Soviet SLBMs also have a higher accuracy than their predecessors. Analysts further suggest that if SLBMs have a high degree of accuracy it would make them less of a retaliatory weapon and would enhance their usefulness for counter-force strikes.[30]

The increased range of, *inter alia,* the Soviet Union's current SS-N-20 on the Typhoon submarine and the SS-N-23 on the Delta-IV allows these submarines on patrol to remain close to or within the Soviet Union's home waters. The Trident missile has a similar range. This means that the survivability of the submarines is increased, which is thought to enhance strategic stability.

As regards the SLCMs, their range and accuracy has considerably improved. Reportedly, the United States is deploying a new vertical launching system (VLS), which is designed to launch anti-submarine, anti-aircraft, anti-ship and land attack missiles from the same set of launching tubes.[31]

On the whole, it appears that the technological developments throughout the 1980s more or less followed the main trends that were evident prior to that period. Thus, no major breakthrough has yet occurred with regard to nuclear-weapon systems, although research work continues in several areas.

While some technological developments — in such areas as remote sensing and the use of satellites — have improved verification capabilities, the development and deployment of weapons systems incorporating advanced technologies have posed more complex problems for verification of nuclear arms limitation and disarmament agreements.

Considering that the Soviet Union and the United States have historically always taken the lead with regard to the technological development of nuclear weapons, it is reasonable to assume that the outcome of their negotiations on the reduction of their strategic nuclear weapons may, in many important aspects, decisively determine both the pace and trends of possible future developments in this field.

D.
Ballistic missile defence systems and countermeasures

Parallel with technological developments in the field of nuclear weapons, at various times efforts were made by nuclear-weapon States to develop defence systems against strategic ballistic missiles carrying nuclear weapons to decrease the effectiveness of such systems.

Both the United States and the Soviet Union carried out research work in this field as early as the 1950s and deployed one anti-ballistic missile system each. While the United States system (which was later dismantled) was deployed for the defence of an ICBM field, the Soviet Union's Galosh system (which still exists) was built around Moscow. In 1972, by mutual agreement, the two sides limited deployment of the systems and placed various restrictions on future development and deployment of anti-ballistic missile systems (see chap. VIII). In 1974 they agreed to limit further such deployments to one site in each country, but only the Soviet Union has chosen to exercise its option under this agreement to maintain an operational ABM site.

For a long time it was suggested that the large phased array radar at Krasnoyarsk was intended not only for early warning of an ICBM attack, but also for ballistic missile detection and tracking. Further, the United States believed the facility could form a critical building block in a nationwide ballistic missile defence (BMD) system that the Soviet Union might have planned, and that it was in violation of the ABM Treaty. In October 1989 Soviet Foreign Minister Eduard Shevardnadze acknowledged that the Krasnoyarsk radar was in violation of the ABM Treaty and stated that it would be dismantled.[32]

Work on various BMD technologies continued and in the 1980s interest in the development of BMD capability was renewed in the United States. This was related, in addition to various political-strategic considerations, to the emergence of new technologies.

At present, research and development of strategic defence systems are progressing in a number of directions, which could lead to systems that might be used against RVs of ICBMs and SLBMs, or against the buses carrying the RVs or against the missiles themselves.[33]

Unlike the situation with earlier ABM weapons, which focused on interception solely during the terminal phase of an RV's flight, interest in new BMD weapons turned in the 1980s to the destruction of ICBMs and SLBMs along their entire trajectory.[34]

There is a whole array of existing and conceptual weapons technologies under consideration for use in BMD. System components could be either ground-, air- or space-based. There are several basic types of new BMD weapons being researched: kinetic energy weapons (KEW), lasers and particle beams.

In a kinetic energy weapon projectiles are hurled at high rates of speed and the force of its impact alone disables or destroys its target. The projectiles could be accelerated by non-conventional means such as electromagnetic "rail-guns".[35]

Another class of potential weapons are lasers, which can be sea-, air-, space- or land-based. If the laser itself is ground-based, the laser beam, theoretically, can be directed onto a target by mirrors based in space.[36]

Another type of potential weapon is based on the use of particle beams. These weapons would accelerate atomic or sub-atomic particles to near the speed of light. The beam would then penetrate the target and disrupt its electronics and other components.[37] There are a number of other technologies that might be used for weapons purposes, although they remain highly theoretical. One is the X-ray laser, which would be pumped by a nuclear explosion. Another is the "plasmoid" defence, which is a cloud of energized atomic nuclei and electrons that affects warheads.

Possible countermeasures include shielding of ICBMs or RVs. In addition, decoy RVs can be installed in ICBMs to distract weapons or cause identification problems for tracking systems. It is also possible to shorten the boost phase of a missile by increasing its speed at launch, thus going a considerable way towards negating the ability of the other side to destroy fully loaded ICBMs before they release their RVs.[38]

In the 1980s, as military satellites became more integrated into military observation, communications and weapon guidance, their importance as targets also increased. Renewed focus on this field also arose as a result of a belief that a number of ballistic missile defence technologies could find an initial application as anti-satellite (ASAT) systems.

Both the United States and Soviet Union have carried on research, development and testing of ASATs. The Soviet Union has tested a co-orbital interceptor ASAT, while the United States has tested an air-launched direct ascent missile.[39] The United States suspended its programme in 1988.

ASATs can be deployed in a variety of ways. They can be used to counter strategic defence. Many satellites would be needed to track, identify and target any incoming ICBMs. The destruction of these satellites would be devastating to nearly all types of BMD systems. ASATs could also be used to attack space-based BMD kill-mechanisms.[40]

There has been considerable debate over the feasibility and merit of the United States strategic defense initiative (SDI) put forward in 1983. The debate has taken place not only between the United States and the Soviet Union, but also between the United States and its allies, within the United States itself, and in many other parts of the world.[41]

The Soviet Union has been carrying out research into technologies that could be used in a BMD system. It has, however, officially declared that it has no integrated large-scale BMD research programme, that all its BMD research is conducted within the limits of the ABM Treaty and that it has no intention to create and to deploy a nation-wide ground-based or space-based BMD.[42]

Notes

1.   See *Study on the Relationship between Disarmament and Development* (United Nations publication, Sales No. E.82.IX.1), paras. 403 and 407.

2.   Thomas B. Cochran, William A. Arkin and Milton M. Hoenig, *Nuclear Weapons Databook: Vol. 1 (US Nuclear Forces)*, Cambridge, Mass., Ballinger Publishers, 1984, pp. 26-28.

3.   The first fusion device detonated by the United States in 1952 had a yield reported to be about 10 Mt. Two years later the United States tested a weapon with a 15 Mt yield, and in 1961 the USSR exploded a fusion weapon with an estimated yield of about 60 Mt.

4.   The first live nuclear artillery test was "Shot Grable", conducted in Nevada on 25 May 1953. See Cochran *et al., op. cit.,* pp. 300 and 301.

5.   See John May, *The Greenpeace Book of the Nuclear Age: The Hidden History, the Human Cost,* New York, Pantheon/Greenpeace Communications Ltd., 1989, pp. 18-25.

6.   Cochran *et al., op. cit.,* pp. 28 and 31.

7.   *Ibid.,* pp. 28 and 29.

8.   For example, the small atomic demolition munition "effectively breaks any barrier between nuclear and conventional explosives if measured purely in terms of yield". See *Guide to Nuclear Weapons 1984-85*, Bradford, School of Peace Studies, University of Bradford, 1984, p. 35.

9.   *Comprehensive Study on Nuclear Weapons* (United Nations publication, Sales No. E.81.I.11), paras. 76 and 85.

10. Cochran *et al., op. cit.,* pp. 172 and 173.

11. *Ibid.,* pp. 31-35.

12. *Ibid.,* p. 319.

13. *Ibid.,* pp. 100-110, especially table 5.11, p. 108.

14. See Richard K. Betts, ed., *Cruise Missiles, Technology, Strategy, Politics,* Washington, Brookings Institution, 1981, pp. 32, 34 and 365-368. See also *Cruise Missiles: Background, Technology and Verification,* Ottawa, Department of External Affairs, 1987, pp. 28 and 29.

15. See Cochran *et al., op. cit.,* pp. 172-190.

16. Sverre Lodgaard and Frank Blackaby, "The nuclear arms race" in *SIPRI Yearbook 1984,* Philadelphia, Taylor and Francis, 1984, pp. 25-29.

17. Here it is necessary to distinguish between ballistic missiles, which are guided mainly during the "boosting" phase, i.e. the initial part of the flight when the rocket engines work; vehicles like cruise missiles, which are driven through the entire flight path and for which guidance becomes navigation; and weapons (of any kind) in their final approach to the target, when target-acquisition and homing devices developed for conventional munitions might be used.

18. See Jeff Hecht, *Beam Weapons,* New York, Plenum Press, 1984, pp. 202 and 203.

19. See May, *op. cit.*

20. War-fighting capability is an elusive term when dealing with nuclear weapons. Proponents of a war-fighting capability argue that without realistic plans to fight and win a nuclear war, deterrence posture cannot be credible. Those who maintain that there can be no winners in a nuclear war, however, see preparations for fighting one as futile and dangerous, since such planning can make nuclear war seem "winnable" and hence more acceptable. This position advocates mutually assured destruction as the basis for a credible deterrence. See Robbin Laird, *The Soviet Union, the West and the Nuclear Arms Race,* New York, New York University Press, 1986, pp. 58-66. See also David Robertson, *Dictionary of Modern Defense and Strategy,* London, Europa, 1987, pp. 317 and 318.

21. Cochran *et al., op. cit.,* p. 116.

22. Bernard Blake, ed., *Jane's Weapons Systems 1988-1989,* Surrey, Jane's Information Group Ltd., 1988, p. 906. See also *SIPRI Yearbook 1988,* p. 53.

23. Blake, *op. cit.,* p. 906.

24. *Jane's Defence Weekly,* 23 June 1990, p. 1234; see also *Flygvapennytt* (Swedish Air Force News), No. 1, 1990.

25. The B-2 is a thick-winged "flying wing", where the wings blend into the fuselage, and radar-absorbing material coats the craft and is attached directly to the metal. See Blake, *op. cit.,* p. 448. See also Jay M. Shafritz, Todd J. A. Shafritz and David B. Robertson, eds., *The Facts on File Dictionary of Military Science,* New York, Facts on File Inc., 1989, p. 434.

26. *IISS Military Balance 1989-90,* IISS, 1989, p. 16. See also Frank Carlucci, *US Secretary of Defense Annual Report to the Congress, Fiscal Year 1990,* Washington, US Government Printing Office, 1989, table III.F.1, p. 184.

27. *SIPRI Yearbook 1990,* Oxford, Oxford University Press, 1990, p. 16. See also *Soviet Military Power,* Washington, US Government Printing Office, 1988, p. 50.

28. *SIPRI Yearbook 1989,* Oxford, Oxford University Press, 1989, p. 21.

29. *Ibid.*, p. 31. See also Commissariat à l'Energie Atomique, *Rapport Annuel 1989*, Paris, CEA, 1990, p. 53.

30. See Blake, *op. cit.*, p. 30.

31. James P. Rubin, "Limiting SLCM's — a better way to START", in *Arms Control Today*, 1989, p. 12. See also Carlucci, *op. cit.*, p. 145.

32. *The New York Times*, p. A1, 24 October 1989.

33. For a more detailed discussion of BMD technologies, see Stephen Weiner, "Systems and technology", in Ashton B. Carter and David N. Schwarz, eds., *Ballistic Missile Defense*, Washington, D.C., Brookings Institution, 1984, pp. 49-97.

34. Ballistic missiles have four phases in their flight profile: (a) boost phase; (b) post-boost phase; (c) mid-course phase; and (d) terminal phase. The success of any defence would depend on which phase of a missile's flight path countermeasures were taken against it and how successful each phase of the defence was in degrading the overall level of an attack. US Department of Defense, Office of Technology Assessment, Heritage Foundation, *Anti-Missile and Anti-Satellite Technologies and Programs, SDI and ASAT*, New Jersey, Noyes Publications, 1986, p. 18.

35. *Anti-Missile and Anti-Satellite Technologies and Programs...*, pp. 16 and 26.

36. *Ibid.*, p. 16.

37. *Ibid.*, pp. 127 and 128.

38. *Ibid.*, pp. 115-119.

39. Satellites have a critical role in providing warning of the launch of any nuclear missile and provide indispensable links in the command and control systems in both crisis and conflict situations. For an in-depth discussion, see Paul B. Stares, "Nuclear operations and antisatellites", in Ashton B. Carter, John D. Steinbruner and Charles A. Zraket, eds., *Managing Nuclear Operations*, Washington, D.C., Brookings Institution, 1987, pp. 679-688.

40. See "Countermeasures, counter-countermeasures, ad infinitum", in Hecht, *op. cit.*, pp. 175-191.

41. See, for example, Harold Brown, ed., *The Strategic Defense Initiative: Shield or Snare?*, Boulder, Westview Press, 1987.

42. "Gorbachev interviewed for United States television", *Facts on File*, New York, Facts on File Inc., December, 1987, pp. 890 and 891; see also *Pravda*, 2 December 1987.

IV
Doctrines and strategies concerning nuclear weapons

A.
General

Military doctrines are developed basically to determine the conditions under which force would be used and as guidelines for force structuring and war plans. Throughout history military doctrines have changed considerably, reflecting changes in perceptions, the evolution of the international environment and the development of different means of warfare. Similarly, various military doctrines relating to the use or threat of use of nuclear weapons have been continuously revised over the past 40 years in conjunction with the changes in the nuclear potentials of the major Powers and the rapid technological developments in the field.

The concept of deterrence is as old as the phenomenon of war. Doctrines of deterrence basically seek to influence the decisions of the opposing side. Thus they rest on the perceptions of the State(s) being deterred. Such a State must be convinced that the other side has at its disposal the military means to support its doctrine and furthermore that there is a "sufficient" likelihood that it would implement it. Generally, deterrence is based on the threat of use of force to prevent someone from carrying out certain hostile acts.

In the nuclear age, however, the notion of deterrence has acquired totally new dimensions. The overwhelmingly destructive power of nuclear weapons has given new potency to the deterrence posture of the nuclear-weapon States. Nuclear deterrence by the threat of massive destruction is based on the idea that if one nuclear-weapon State launches an attack on another nuclear-weapon State, the defender will have sufficient force left after the attack in order to be able to launch a retaliatory strike that would inflict unacceptable damage on the aggressor.[1] Thus, according to this concept, the aggressor would be dissuaded from initiating an attack. The question of nuclear deterrence takes on particular significance at the regional level with respect to those States which reportedly possess nuclear warheads or nuclear explosive devices and which, at the same time, are not parties to the Treaty on the

Non-Proliferation of Nuclear Weapons. It relates also to the possibility that nuclear weapons could be used to threaten and endanger the security of a region and of neighbouring States, creating for them the need to devise appropriate security arrangements on which they can rely (see chap. III).

Several fundamental issues have been debated more or less since the inception of the nuclear age. One is whether nuclear weapons are indispensable for an effective deterrence. Another is whether they can deter conventional attack or only nuclear attack.[2] Major uncertainty also surrounds critically important questions under what circumstances a certain State would in fact use its nuclear weapons.[3] In this connection, there are those who believe that one cannot say with assurance that reality will unfold according to expectations based on the existing doctrines and that one cannot disregard the possibility of events developing independently of the professed doctrines.

Other issues raised are whether or not a nuclear-weapon State can credibly extend nuclear deterrence to its allies ("extended deterrence"); whether an assured retaliatory capability is sufficient for deterrence ("minimum deterrence") or if this calls for larger and more varied forces, i.e. a "war-fighting" capability; and, finally, whether deterrence in reality rests on the mere existence of powerful nuclear arsenals ("existential deterrence"). If that is the case, even quite large differences in the size of the arsenals, as well as refinements in technology and employment concepts, would be largely irrelevant. The question still remains as to how much and what type of nuclear weaponry are sufficient for deterrence. In the view of many, this has, in the past, led to an arms race resulting in excessive nuclear arsenals.

Different States assess nuclear weapons and deterrence differently. There are those who believe that nuclear deterrence has played an important role in preventing the outbreak of a world conflict and that nuclear deterrence will continue to be a prerequisite for international stability and world security for the foreseeable future. Others consider that the risks of a failure of deterrence are too high to be worth taking, since nuclear war could cause intolerable destruction in any part of the globe, no matter how distant from the centre of conflict. They believe that nuclear weapons should be banned and abolished and that viable security alternatives must be considered on the basis of broad multilateral co-operation rather than on a permanent adversarial relationship.

The views on nuclear-weapon doctrines, including deterrence, are described briefly in section D of the present chapter. More detailed discussions are presented in the United Nations *Study on Deterrence*.[4] The five nuclear-weapon States have submitted, for publication in the present study, short descriptions of their doctrinal views on the use of nuclear weapons. These are given in appendix I.

The following section describes briefly the main features of the nuclear doctrines of the nuclear-weapon States. These doctrines have historically evolved and there has also been a fair amount of interaction between different doctrines, either through the process of negotiations on arms limitation or through changing perceptions of threats to the national security of those countries. A great deal of the evolution of and interaction between doctrines may be attributed to developments of weapon technologies.

B.
Doctrines of the nuclear-weapon States
1.
The United States

Although it was recognized in the United States during the immediate post-war years that the atomic bomb might potentially change all military strategy, no particular doctrine had emerged at that time for the use of this weapon. The bomb was viewed mainly as a somewhat bigger weapon to be used in the same way other bombs had been used. By 1948, strategic air strikes figured prominently in United States Air Force nuclear war planning.[5]

At the end of the 1940s and the beginning of the 1950s, under the impact of the changing world situation and the development of the Soviet Union's nuclear capability, a re-evaluation of American defence policy was begun, which affected both the level of nuclear armaments and military doctrine. The United States Strategic Air Command, which had been given overall responsibility for target planning for nuclear weapons use, recommended that, owing to the small size of the available arsenal and the paucity of reliable intelligence on Soviet infrastructure targets, counter-city nuclear strikes would be militarily more effective than attacks on the energy and transportation infrastructure. The Korean War had prompted a major United States military effort and President Truman authorized an expansion of nuclear weapons production. The United States stockpile rose from 50 in mid-1948 to about 1,000 in 1953 and reached almost 18,000 by the end of the decade.[6]

At the doctrinal level, in 1954 the United States Secretary of State, John Foster Dulles, announced what was referred to as "the doctrine of massive retaliation". The United States, according to Dulles, reserved the option of retaliating instantly, "by means, at times, and at places of our choosing".[7] That declaration was said to be intended primarily to underscore the preventive nature of the nuclear threat. It did not imply that the United States would automatically bomb the industrial or population centres of an adversary in the event of an attack on the United States or its allies. The United States would not necessarily have to meet military action where it occurred, but might instead respond, with or without nuclear weapons, with attacks on strategic targets.

The first Soviet thermonuclear test in 1953 and the launching of the first Soviet Sputnik in 1957 made it clear that the United States could be exposed to nuclear strikes. This put an end to the idea of the traditional "Fortress America" and also prompted re-evaluation of the doctrine of "massive retaliation". The question was raised: if there was to be some lower level of conflict involving the Soviet Union, should the only available United States response be all-out war, particularly when it could mean mutual suicide?

The need for a revised strategy was recognized by President Eisenhower and further addressed by the Kennedy Administration. Two developments took place. The first was the adoption of the single integrated operational plan (SIOP), which sought to co-ordinate nuclear planning and delivery between the various American armed services.[8] Secondly, NATO's conventional forces were strengthened, presumably to avoid as long as possible recourse to nuclear weapons. The introduction of tactical nuclear weapons in the late 1950s and the emergence of the concept of limited nuclear warfare were two convergent factors of readjustment at the level of military doctrine.

The resulting NATO doctrine took the form of the concept of "flexible response". It was put forward in the beginning of the 1960s by United States Secretary of Defense Robert McNamara. "Flexible response" presumed that NATO would maintain its standing conventional forces at a level at which it could withstand attack by the Warsaw Treaty Organization until reserves were mobilized. Nuclear weapons would be used only if the West faced defeat in a conventional war. This required the existence of flexible and effective conventional forces, if necessary supported by tactical nuclear weapons and ultimately by strategic forces. The doctrine stated that each case of aggression would be dealt with independently and American nuclear response could be controlled for varying levels of response to aggression.[9]

A retaliatory response could be as small as one tactical nuclear charge or as large as a multi-target strike on the Soviet Union. Thus, the Soviet Union would be deterred from attacking since a conflict would run the risk of escalating to an all-out nuclear war.[10] The United States would deploy its nuclear forces in a structure and in sufficient numbers to enable it to ride out a possible first strike by the Soviet Union and then retaliate with enough nuclear forces to destroy one fifth to one fourth of the Soviet population and one half to two thirds of the Soviet industry ("assured destruction").[11] Secretary of Defense McNamara also initially proposed a counter-force strategy. A counter-force attack is an attack aimed at an adversary's military capability, especially its nuclear forces; a counter-value attack is directed against an opponent's civilian and economic centres. However, the technically feasible options of the time offered limited possibilities of reaching and concentrating on military targets. With further technological developments this option gained in importance.

The problem of developing credible options was again elaborated by the Nixon Administration, which sought to create a set of "limited nuclear options" and thus enhance in-conflict escalation control. According to some sources, in 1974 a plan was outlined for the employment of nuclear weapons in a way that would allow the United States to "conduct selected nuclear operations".[12] This approach was reportedly reconfirmed and further developed by the Carter Administration, although Secretary of Defense Harold Brown stressed that "assured destruction" continued to form the "bedrock" of nuclear deterrence.[13] The improvements in the accuracy of missiles and in command and control facilities during the past two decades have stimulated interest in the concept of "selected nuclear operations" and nuclear warfighting.

In 1982, the States parties to the North Atlantic Treaty reaffirmed in a Declaration that none of their weapons, nuclear or conventional, would ever be used except in response to attack.[14]

Perhaps the most significant doctrinal development in the 1980s was the United States' initiative for developing a system of strategic defence (SDI). Basically, the proponents of the idea are endeavouring to deter aggression by denying a potential adversary the certainty that his nuclear strike would succeed. They believe that deterrence would thus become more defensive and less nuclear.[15]

2.
The Soviet Union

After the Second World War, although the Soviet Union was aware of the potential of nuclear weapons, this did not seem to have much effect on its military doctrine. Nuclear weapons were treated simply as bigger explosives.

In 1960, the Chairman of the Soviet Council of Ministers, Nikita Khrushchev, announced that a new branch of the Soviet military forces had been formed — the strategic rocket forces. He also announced that the conventional forces would be reduced or replaced, because nuclear weapons "had made it possible to raise our country's defensive power to such a level that we are capable of making further reduction of our military forces".[16]

In 1961 Defence Minister Malinovsky stated that one of the most important points of the Soviet military doctrine was that a world war — if initiated by an aggressor — "inevitably would take the form of a nuclear missile war".[17] This was an indication that the concepts of deterrence and massive retaliation began to play an important role in Soviet thinking at the time.

These and other statements were followed in 1962 by the publication in the Soviet Union of a comprehensive work on military strategy edited by Marshal V. D. Sokolovsky, which recognized the revolutionary impact of the appearance of nuclear weapons on military strategy. One central thesis in this work was that a war where the two major Powers were involved would inevitably escalate to a general nuclear war:

> "It should be emphasized that, with the international relations existing under present-day conditions and the present level of development of military equipment, any armed conflict will inevitably escalate into a general nuclear war if the nuclear Powers are drawn into this conflict".[18]

Based on this assumption, the Soviet Union attempted in parallel to build up its strategic nuclear forces creating an ability, if necessary, to deliver a credible strike in case of war.

When the concept of "flexible response" was adopted by NATO in 1967, the Soviet views on total nuclear war also started to change gradually. Nuclear weapons were still depicted as a decisive element of war, but it was maintained that only with conventional combined arms operations could the war be won. Beginning in 1965-1966, the Soviet Union apparently began to consider that nuclear war could remain geographically limited. The new edition of Marshal Sokolovsky's work on military strategy supported an increasingly flexible view of the use of nuclear weapons, thus indicating possibilities other than simply massive strategic retaliation:

"In working out the forms and methods for conducting a future war, an entire number of questions should be considered: how will the war be unleashed, what character will it assume, who will be the main enemy, will nuclear weapons be employed at the very start of the war or in the course of the war, which nuclear weapons — strategic or only operational-tactical — where, in what area or in what theatre will the main events unfold, etc".[19]

Eventually, Soviet doctrine underwent further changes. It subsequently held that a war would not inevitably become nuclear. Thus, the Soviet military writer Colonel-General A. S. Zjoltov wrote in 1972 that "it is completely possible that a war can be conducted with only conventional weapons".[20] He said that war without nuclear weapons was possible; even if nuclear weapons were used, these weapons could not solve all military tasks; the use of nuclear weapons against some targets might prove not operative; nuclear weapons could under some circumstances be an obstacle for the advancement of a country's own forces; and that many conventional weapons could be used with great effect against the nuclear weapons of an enemy.

In 1976, it was stated at the highest level in the Soviet Union that "if all presently accumulated nuclear stockpiles were used, humanity would be totally destroyed".[21] In 1981, the Soviet Union announced that victory in nuclear war would be impossible, a sentiment it has expressed ever since. In 1982, the Soviet Union officially declared that it would not be the first to use nuclear weapons in any conflict. It stated that it would not seek to use nuclear weapons since any use, no matter how limited, could lead to escalation to all-out nuclear war. Nevertheless, the Soviet Union continued the expansion of its strategic nuclear forces, which, according to the Soviet Union, took into account the need to ensure their survivability.

The Declaration adopted in 1987 by the Soviet Union and other States parties to the Warsaw Treaty Organization envisaged a new alliance military doctrine subordinated to the task of preventing war, whether nuclear or conventional. Military means to resolve any disputes were said to be inadmissible in the nuclear age. The Declaration pointed out that the defensive nature of their military doctrine resided in the undertakings of the Warsaw Treaty States that they:

a.   would never, under any circumstances, initiate military action unless they were themselves the target of an armed attack;

b.   would not be the first to use nuclear weapons;

c.   did not have any territorial claims to any other State; and

d.   did not view any State or any people as their enemy.[22]

Despite the significant improvements in the international situation and in Soviet-American relations, the Soviet Union considers that it has to take into account in its defence structure, including its strategic arms structure, the considerable military potential of the United States and NATO. For the strategic nuclear forces of the Soviet Union, the essence of defence sufficiency is determined by the need to maintain those forces in such quantity and quality as to provide reliable retaliation capability against nuclear attack upon it in any circumstances, even the most unfavourable. The Soviet Union maintains that it does not seek military supremacy over the United States and does not lay claim to greater security, but at the same time it is fully resolved not to allow the latter to gain military supremacy over it.

The Soviet Union believes that the strategic balance that has developed between the nuclear forces of the USSR and those of the United States, both in the overall quantity of strategic nuclear weapons and in their real operational potential, makes possible in any circumstances to inflict unacceptable damage on the aggressor in a retaliatory (second) strike. The Soviet Union has stated that it is in favour of curbing the nuclear arms race through the contractual lowering of the levels of nuclear weapons. In reducing strategic nuclear weapons, emphasis should be placed on enhancing strategic stability through strengthening their invulnerability while reducing their overall quantity and thus retaining these weapons as effective means of retaliation but not of attack (first strike).

3.
The United Kingdom

The United Kingdom remains fully integrated in NATO. As a member of NATO, the United Kingdom is covered by the United States' extended deterrence. Even though the United Kingdom's nuclear forces are committed to NATO's policy of flexible response, the United Kingdom's possession of its own nuclear weapons gives it an option to initiate independently a nuclear response to attack. These two roles would complicate the strategic responses of a potential aggressor.

Although the United Kingdom's Lance tactical nuclear missiles are under a dual-key system with the United States, its other forces are controlled by the United Kingdom alone. British nuclear weapons are deployed both on British soil and in the Federal Republic of Germany.[23] During a European conflict and where British nuclear weapons were to be used as part of NATO forces, the Supreme Allied Commander in Europe, an American, needs British approval to order the use of British nuclear weapons.[24]

British strategic doctrine is based on what is commonly known as minimum deterrence. In view of the relatively limited number of strategic warheads at its disposal, at present some 128, the doctrine is presumed to be almost purely counter-value.[25]

Most of Britain's forces are targeted on the Soviet Union. In 1962 Britain dedicated its Polaris force to NATO as a strategic deterrent to publicly underline the focus of its nuclear forces.[26] The United Kingdom's strategic nuclear forces ensure that it could "inflict a blow so destructive that the penalty for aggression would have proved too high".[27]

4.
France

Along with the process of withdrawing its military forces from NATO control in 1966, France was developing the essentials of its autonomous national doctrine of nuclear deterrence. France maintains an independent nuclear force, since it believes such a force to be essential for its defence and independence.

France's nuclear strategy is one of *dissuasion du faible au fort,* or the weak deterring the strong. Deterrence and security rest on the threat of nuclear retaliation against a conventional or nuclear attack on France.

According to French declarations, if France felt its vital interests were threatened, it would launch a nuclear "last warning" toward the attacking State. Should the aggressor persist in his actions, this shot would be the precursor of a devastating nuclear attack against France's opponent. Since France's nuclear doctrine is well publicized, the purpose of the ultimate warning would be that the attacker could then determine that the benefits gained by pursuing the attack on France would be far inferior to the costs incurred by doing so.[28]

Originally French nuclear strategy was defined as being aimed at defending French territory. Subsequently, France indicated that it was aimed at defending the vital interests of France. France stresses that the decision to use its nuclear weapons can, by definition, only be made on the sole basis of its national sovereignty. To fulfil its nuclear strategy, the French triad ensures a survivable second-strike capability that is seen as reducing the likelihood of a pre-emptive strike against France.[29]

5.
China

When China first acquired a nuclear-weapon capability, it announced that China would never be the first to use nuclear weapons, and would not, in any circumstances, use nuclear weapons against a non-nuclear-weapon State.[30] However, China's nuclear weapons employment strategy remains largely unknown.

China's defence policy was based for many years on the concept of a "people's war" on the one hand and nuclear deterrence on the other. In the 1960s the people's war concept dominated. According to Mao Zedong, an attack on China, whether nuclear or conventional, would have to be followed by an invasion of ground forces, and this is where the supremacy of the concept of the people's war would be felt. Hostile forces would be lured deep into China's territory, "bogged down in endless battles and drowned in a hostile human sea".[31]

As a result, the Chinese seemed to have opted for a minimal nuclear deterrent. In addition, in spite of a renewed emphasis on its regular military forces, China continued to promote the idea of "peasant armies", which, owing to their size and dispersal, could not be wiped out by nuclear attacks. The Chinese force structure supporting its nuclear doctrine, however, was reported to be pragmatic and flexible.[32]

During the last years of the 1970s, it seemed that the adherents of the concept that in war men are more important than weapons had lost ground. Furthermore, there were indications that efforts were under way to develop more modern general-purpose forces in order to meet more limited military contingencies than the extremes of nuclear deterrence or mass war. There were also indications that China was interested in developing tactical nuclear weapons.[33]

It appears that currently in China, the modernization of existing nuclear-weapon systems takes precedence over a dramatic quantitative build-up of nuclear forces.[34]

C.
Relationship between nuclear weapons, non-nuclear weapons and deterrence

The relationship between nuclear and non-nuclear weapons and its impact on military doctrines is crucial to an examination of the concept of deterrence.

The discussion regarding this relationship has centred chiefly on the situation prevailing in Europe where the two military alliances, NATO and the Warsaw Treaty Organization, have over the years faced one another with a large concentration of forces, both nuclear and conventional. Notwithstanding this concentration on Europe, similar points could be drawn in relation to the Sino-Soviet nuclear balance and indeed to maritime strategy in the Pacific.

On the NATO side, the perceived superiority of the Soviet Union and the Warsaw Treaty countries with regard to conventional forces has long been a focal point of a debate on the overall balance of forces, including the role of nuclear weapons in the maintenance of a credible deterrent posture in Europe. The doctrine of flexible response presupposes the existence of conventional forces sufficiently strong to provide the NATO alliance with options other than those of defeat or an early nuclear response. At the same time, NATO has considered it necessary to retain the possibility of a first use of nuclear weapons at least as long as the perceived conventional imbalance has not been rectified and the other side possesses large and flexible nuclear forces. In a policy declaration, the North Atlantic Council Meeting held at Brussels in May 1989 stated in its communiqué that "the Allies' sub-strategic nuclear forces are not meant to compensate for conventional imbalances".[35] In June 1990, NATO foreign ministers stated that "for the foreseeable future, the prevention of war will require an appropriate mix of survivable and effective conventional and nuclear forces at the lowest levels consistent with our security needs".[36]

The debate on the need to further reduce incentives for the early use of nuclear weapons in a major war in Europe has continued during the 1980s. In 1979 the United States decided to reduce its stockpile of tactical nuclear weapons in Europe. At the NATO meeting at Montebello in 1983, decisions were taken on the further restructuring of NATO's forces, including an agreement to withdraw a total of 1,400 tactical nuclear warheads from existing stockpiles.[37]

The Soviet Union holds that its military doctrine has traditionally stressed the importance of both non-nuclear and nuclear weapons as elements of an effective military posture. Over the years, the emphasis of these components has varied, reflecting the evolution in the Soviet overall concept of military strategy as well as its perceptions of the threats to its national security. This pertains to the European theatre in particular, which throughout the post-war period has remained the primary theatre of operations in Soviet military planning. In recent times, Soviet military doctrine has elaborated a new approach towards determining the strength of armed forces, their structure and military construction as a whole that is being put into effect. The Soviet Union has stated that in dealing with these issues it proceeds from the principle of reasonable sufficiency for defence.[38]

With regard to strategic offensive weapons, this principle, according to the Soviet Union, requires maintenance of the approximate balance in such weapons between the Soviet Union and the United States. Their structure may differ, but their potential combat capability at any level of reductions should be comparable.

The Soviet position is that, for conventional armed forces, sufficiency for defence implies a level of battle strength at which they are capable of repelling possible aggression, but, at the same time, not capable of carrying out an attack and conducting large-scale offensive operations. This means giving armed forces a non-offensive structure; limiting the number of strike-weapon systems; changing the groupings of armed forces and their deployment, with the aim of enhancing their capabilities for defence; and lowering the levels of military production, military expenditure and military activities as a whole.

The Soviet Union has announced that the structure of its Armed Forces is being reorganized in a defensive spirit, as follows. Apart from unilateral reductions in its Armed Forces by 500,000 men (to be completed by the end of 1990) the number of military regions, armies and general military divisions has been reduced. The correlation between means of offence and means of defence is being changed in favour of the latter. Operational manoeuvre groups and concentrated tank groupings have been disbanded. Those Soviet divisions still remaining for the present in the territories of the allies of the Soviet Union are being reorganized.[39] A large number of tanks are being withdrawn from these divisions (40 per cent of those in the motorized infantry divisions and 20 per cent of those in the tank divisions) and taken out of service. The divisions are being given a defensive structure.[40]

Following the unilateral withdrawal of some 500 tactical nuclear weapons from Europe in 1989, the Soviet Union announced that it was willing to make further significant reductions of its tactical nuclear missiles as soon as the NATO countries would formally agree to start negotiations on tactical nuclear weapons in Europe. It also reiterated its proposals to include the issue of short-range nuclear forces in the agenda on disarmament and arms reduction in Europe. In April 1990, NATO agreed to start negotiations on tactical nuclear weapons after the conclusion of an agreement on conventional force reductions in Europe (CFE).

The progress in the CFE negotiations at Vienna, the Soviet conventional force reductions, the restructuring of Soviet and other Warsaw Treaty country forces in a more defensive direction, following the adoption in 1987 of a new military doctrine of the Alliance, as well as the withdrawal of some United States tactical nuclear warheads from Europe, are developments with potentially far-reaching implications for traditional force postures in Europe.

The highest representatives of the Warsaw Pact member States, gathered in Moscow on 7 June 1990 for a meeting of the political consultative committee, stated, *inter alia*: "Participants in the meeting are unanimous in their opinion that the ideological enemy image has been overcome by mutual efforts of the East and the West". They further stated: "Confrontation elements contained in documents of the Warsaw Treaty and the North Atlantic Treaty Organization that were adopted in the past are no longer in line with the spirit of the time" (see A/45/312, annex).

At the July 1990 North Atlantic Council meeting of Heads of State and Government, a Declaration was adopted in which it was stated, *inter alia*, that the Alliance "will never in any circumstances be the first to use force". Furthermore, the Declaration stated the following:[41]

> "The political and military changes in Europe, and the prospects of further changes, now allow the Allies concerned to go further. They will thus modify the size and adapt the tasks of their nuclear deterrent forces. They have concluded that, as a result of the new political and military conditions in Europe, there will be a significantly reduced role for sub-strategic nuclear systems of the shortest range. They have decided specifically that, once negotiations begin on short-range nuclear forces, the Alliance will propose, in return for reciprocal action by the Soviet Union, the elimination of all its nuclear artillery shells from Europe.

> "New negotiations between the United States and the Soviet Union on the reduction of short-range nuclear forces should begin shortly after a CFE agreement is signed. The Allies concerned will develop an arms control framework for these negotiations which takes into account our requirements for far fewer nuclear weapons, and the diminished need for sub-strategic nuclear systems of the shortest range.

> "Finally, with the total withdrawal of Soviet stationed forces and the implementation of a CFE agreement, the Allies concerned can reduce their reliance on nuclear weapons. These will continue to fulfil an essential role in the overall strategy of the Alliance to prevent war by ensuring that there are no circumstances in which nuclear retaliation in response to military action might be discounted. However, in the transformed Europe, they will be able to adopt a new NATO strategy making nuclear forces truly weapons of last resort.

> "We approve the mandate given in Turnberry to the North Atlantic Council in Permanent Session to oversee the ongoing work on the adaptation of the Alliance to the new circumstances. It should report its conclusion as soon as possible.

> "In the context of these revised plans for defence and arms control,

and with the advice of NATO Military Authorities and all member States concerned, NATO will prepare a new Allied military strategy moving away from 'forward defence', where appropriate, towards a reduced forward presence and modifying 'flexible response' to reflect a reduced reliance on nuclear weapons. In that connection, NATO will elaborate new force plans consistent with the revolutionary changes in Europe. NATO will also provide a forum for Allied consultation on the upcoming negotiations on short-range nuclear forces."

D.
Differing positions regarding nuclear deterrence

Depending on the attitude regarding nuclear weapons and the role of these weapons in international relations, schools of thought on the subject range from acceptance by necessity to total rejection of nuclear weapons (see United Nations *Study on Deterrence*).

Proponents of deterrence maintain that deterrence is not just a Western position but a universal concept. They believe that the success of nuclear deterrence is a political and strategic fact of the post-war period. It has been deemed necessary for constraining the offensive use of military forces and for resisting possible military and political intimidation by a potential opponent. Thus, in their opinion, nuclear deterrence is an exclusively defensive strategy and represents the best means of maintaining stability.[42]

The existence of nuclear deterrence, they believe, has not only preserved the European continent from an East-West armed conflict, but has also led to a historic break with the process of confrontation, which frequently gave rise to armed conflicts. In their opinion, no system of security has been able up to now to offer guarantees similar to those provided by nuclear deterrence. They maintain that deterrence is also fully compatible with the principle of self-defence recognized by the Charter of the United Nations.[43]

Furthermore, they also believe that conventional warfare, which since the Second World War has decimated populations in many parts of the world with increasingly destructive weapons, is no more moral than nuclear non-warfare. Consequently, nuclear deterrence cannot be judged in moral or ethical terms without taking into account what they consider the most relevant criterion in this respect, that of stability: past, present and future. The world is no less secure today than in 1914 or 1939 when nuclear weapons were unknown.[44]

The critics of nuclear deterrence point out that nuclear weapons are weapons of mass destruction radically different from any other weapons mankind has previously known. They are weapons that defy traditional concepts of strategy. Any nuclear-weapon State that relies on nuclear deterrence, they believe, must ultimately be prepared to employ its weapons. They contend that military response, according to international law, must not be out of proportion with an armed attack. The use of nuclear weapons in response to a conventional attack would be, however, inherently a disproportionate response. Furthermore, their use would entail a risk of escalation to an all-out nuclear war, which would mean not only the total destruction of combatants, but also a threat to the survival of non-nuclear-weapon States and, in the end, of all mankind. The order of damage likely in a nuclear conflict would be beyond all historical experience.[45] The overwhelming majority of non-nuclear-weapon States have rejected nuclear weapons and related doctrines as a means for their security.

A basic conceptual difficulty associated with the doctrine of nuclear deterrence in the opinion of its critics is that it continues to expound the utility of the possession of nuclear weapons and their possible use. Since all States have equal rights to security, such an approach, they argue, runs counter to desired objectives of nuclear nonproliferation, particularly in an environment of improved international relations. In addition, critics argue that it is not possible to prove that nuclear deterrence is to be credited with the maintenance of peace in Europe. In any case, the risk of nuclear war is unacceptable to them (see chap. VII). Furthermore, they believe that in some cases the possession of nuclear weapons complicates the solution of international problems, particularly at the regional level. A country that possesses nuclear weapons and is not a party to the Non-Proliferation Treaty will rely on such weapons, for purposes of intimidation or if necessary for use, as long as regional problems remain unsolved, and it will do so in its dealings with parties that do not have nuclear capabilities for warlike purposes. In such a case, nuclear deterrence thus becomes a significant factor militating against the integrity of certain regions.

Other criticisms include the issue of rationality. Critics contend that misperception of the other side's motives, miscalculation or even accidental launch of weaponry could remove weapons from rational control.

Notes   1.   The concept of unacceptable damage was introduced by United States Secretary of Defense Robert McNamara in the 1960s and defined as destruction of 20 per cent of the Soviet population and 50 per cent of industrial capacity. Subsequently many theorists have contended that the destruction by a nuclear strike on even a few major cities would constitute "unacceptable damage" for that country. There is no precise method of measuring levels of destruction to include the effects of fall-out, general social disruption, etc. Lawrence Freedman, *The Evolution of Nuclear Strategy*, New York, St. Martin's Press, 1989, pp. 246 and 247.

2.   *Study on Deterrence* (United Nations publication, Sales No. E.87.IX.2).

3.   See David Robertson, *Dictionary of Modern Defense and Strategy*, London, Europa Publications Ltd., 1987, pp. 133 and 134.

4.   See *Study on Deterrence, op. cit.*

5.   David Alan Rosenberg, "The origins of overkill: nuclear weapons in American strategy 1945-60", in Steven E. Miller, ed., *Strategy and Nuclear Deterrence*, Princeton, Princeton University Press, 1984, pp. 124-127.

6.   *Ibid.*, pp. 124-133.

7.   John Foster Dulles, "The evolution of foreign policy", in *The Department of State Bulletin*, vol. 30, 25 January 1954, p. 108.

8.   The first SIOP, formally designated SIOP-62, was completed in December 1960 and officially entered into effect on 1 July 1961 (i.e. the beginning of fiscal year 1962). Since then there have been SIOP-63 (in 1962), SIOP-5 (in 1976) and SIOP-6 (in 1983).

9.   See Robin Laird, *The Soviet Union, the West and the Nuclear Arms Race*, New York, New York University Press, 1986, p. 49. See also Alexander L. George and Richard Smoke, eds., *Deterrence in American Foreign Policy*, New York, Columbia University Press, 1974, pp. 31 and 32.

10.   A ladder of escalation is used to describe the course that a crisis would take as it proceeded from the lowest levels of conflict (diplomacy and sanctions) to all-out nuclear war and mutual annihilation. Depending on the seriousness of the situation, a State may respond to an attack with what it regards as appropriate means, which may be conventional weapons, tactical nuclear weapons or various modes of employment of strategic nuclear weapons.

11.   Desmond Ball, "The development of the SIOP, 1960-1983", in *Strategic Nuclear Targeting*, Desmond Ball and Jeffrey Richelson, eds., Ithaca, New York, Cornell University Press, 1986, p. 69.

12.   See Laird, *op. cit.*, pp. 58-64.

13.   Desmond Ball, *op. cit.*, pp. 76-79. See also Committee on Foreign Relations, *Nuclear War Strategy: Hearing Before the Committee on Foreign Relations, US Senate, 96th Congress, 2nd session, on Presidential Directive 59, 16 September 1980*, Washington, US Government Printing Office, 1981.

14.   *NATO Review*, vol. 30, No. 3, 1982, pp. 25-27.

15.   See, for example, Paul Nitze, "On the road to a more stable peace?", in P. Edward Haley and Jack Merritt, eds., *Strategic Defense Initiative, Folly or Future?*, Boulder, Westview Press, 1986, pp. 37-41.

16.   *Pravda*, 15 January 1960.

17.   *Pravda*, 25 October 1961.

18.   V. D. Sokolovsky, *Soviet Military Strategy* (English translation), MacDonald and Jane's, London, 1975, p. 195.

19. *Ibid.*, p. 288.
20. A. S. Zjoltov, *Militärische Theorie und Militärische Praxis,* Berlin, Militärverlag der DDR, 1972.
21. From a speech of Leonid Brezhnev in Bucharest, *Pravda,* 25 November 1976.
22. See document A/42/313-S/18888.
23. Peter Malone, *The British Nuclear Deterrent,* New York, St. Martin's Press, 1984, pp. 92 and 94.
24. *Ibid.*, pp. 93-95.
25. *SIPRI Yearbook 1990,* Oxford, Oxford University Press, p. 20.
26. Malone, *op. cit.,* p. 93.
27. United Kingdom Ministry of Defence, *The Future United Kingdom Strategic Nuclear Deterrence Force,* Defence Open Government Document 80/23, London, HMSO, 1980, p. 5.
28. David Yost, "French nuclear targeting", in Ball and Richelson, eds., *op. cit.* p. 134.
29. *Ibid.*, p. 106.
30. George Segal, "Nuclear forces", in George Segal and William T. Tow, eds., *Chinese Defense Policy,* Urbana, University of Illinois Press, 1984, p. 99.
31. Ralph L. Powell, "Maoist military doctrine", in *Asian Survey,* April 1968.
32. Segal, *op. cit.,* pp. 100-109.
33. *Ibid.*, p. 106.
34. Economic reforms emphasizing the civilian sector and improved relations with the USSR may have led to a decrease in China's pursuit of quantitative improvements in its nuclear weapons programmes. See *SIPRI Yearbook 1988,* p. 52. See also *SIPRI Yearbook 1989,* p. 34.
35. "A Comprehensive Concept of Arms Control and Disarmament", adopted by Heads of State and Government at the meeting of the North Atlantic Council at Brussels on 29 and 30 May 1989 (A/44/481, annex II).
36. See Conference on Disarmament document CD/1006, para. 11.
37. Ivo Daalder, "NATO nuclear targeting and the INF Treaty", in *Journal of Strategic Studies,* vol. 11, September 1988, p. 279.
38. See "On the military doctrine of the Soviet Union", statement of the Chief of General Staff of the Armed Forces of the USSR General of the Army, M. A. Moiseev, at the Vienna seminar of 35 States on military doctrines, 16 January 1990.
39. By 1991 all Soviet troops are to be withdrawn from Hungary and most likely Czechoslovakia as well. The future of Soviet troops on East German soil remains to be seen, but it appears certain that they will undergo reductions from their present level of approximately 380,000 troops.
40. See *SIPRI Yearbook 1989,* "The Soviet military and perestroika", pp. 24 and 25.
41. See Conference on Disarmament document CD/1013, paras. 16-20.
42. See, *inter alia,* Christopher Achen and Duncan Snidal, "Rational deterrence theory and comparative case studies", in *World Politics,* vol. 41, January 1989, pp. 143-169.
43. See Amos J. Peaslee, *International Governmental Organizations Constitutional Documents,* Part One, The Hague, Martinus Nühoff, 1974, pp. 1310 and 1311.

44.   See, *inter alia,* Bernard Brodie, "The development of nuclear strategy", in Miller, *op. cit.,* p. 14.

45.   See Julio Carasales, "Chapter I", *Study on Deterrence* (United Nations publication, Sales No. E.87.IX.2).

V
Development, production and testing of nuclear weapons

A.
Decision-making regarding the development and testing of nuclear weapons

The international community is divided on the issue of the possession of nuclear weapons. The overwhelming majority of States have refrained from acquiring such weapons. More than 45 years after the first nuclear devices were developed, only a small number of States have acquired nuclear arms. Significantly, more than 130 States, including three nuclear-weapon States, in the Final Declaration of the 1985 Third Review Conference of the Non-Proliferation Treaty, declared their continued support for the prevention of proliferation of nuclear weapons or other nuclear explosive devices.[1] It appears, therefore, that the vast majority of States believes that acquisition of nuclear weapons would not serve their security interests and that emergence of additional nuclear-weapon States is liable to have considerable regional, or even global, security ramifications (see chaps. VII and VIII).

A decision to develop, build and test a nuclear weapon is complex. Following a political decision to acquire nuclear weapons, a non-nuclear-weapon State must develop the required technologies and ensure the supply of nuclear fissile material. Considerable research, development, engineering and industrial capacity are required to build facilities either to make enriched uranium or to extract plutonium from spent reactor fuel. To build such facilities is a complex and expensive task, which is beyond the domestic capabilities of many countries.

After the decision has been made as to how to acquire the fissile material, a State must decide whether to test its developed weapon. It is probable that a workable first-generation fission weapon could be developed without testing, although it is uncertain how reliable this device would be. The Hiroshima bomb was not tested, and design and construction may well be easier today with the use of supercomputers. To develop advanced nuclear weapons, such as fusion weapons, would, however, require testing.

61

B.
Nuclear testing and its relationship to the continued development of warheads

The testing of nuclear warheads is a critical element in the production of nuclear weapons, because each new type of nuclear weapon typically requires the development of a new warhead. It is believed that most testing is done to develop specific new warheads, with half a dozen explosions required to develop a brand new design. Further tests are conducted to check weapons as they come off the production line, and also for their reliability when they reach the stockpile.[2] Nuclear-test explosions are also used to research new kinds of nuclear weapons. "Weapons effects" tests are also carried out to measure the effect of radiation on military equipment. Most details of nuclear tests are kept secret.

All five nuclear-weapon States conduct nuclear tests as part of their weapons programmes. Between 1945 and 1989 there were 1,819 internationally recorded tests (an average of one test every nine days) with a total yield of many hundred megatons (see table 1). Testing has been carried out on every continent except South America and Antarctica, as well as on a number of island territories in the Pacific Ocean. The United States, the Soviet Union and China test at isolated sites within their respective mainlands. The United Kingdom uses the American test site in Nevada. France has two test sites in French Polynesia.

Table 1
Recent nuclear testing data[3]

Country	First test	Current test site	Number of tests				
			1986	1987	1988	1989	All tests
United States	1945	Nevada	14	14	14	11	921
Union of Soviet Socialist Republics	1949	Semipalatinsk/ Novaya Zemlya	0[a]	23	17	7	642
United Kingdom	1952	Nevada	1	1	0	1	42
France	1960	Mururoa/ Fangataufa	8	8	8	8	180
China	1964	Lop Nor, Sinkiang	0	1	1	0	34

[a]   The USSR held a moratorium on testing August 1985 – February 1987.

Except for a few underwater tests, the early tests were carried out in the atmosphere, provoking widespread concern about the effects of radioactive fall-out. Since the 1963 Treaty Banning Nuclear Weapon Tests in the Atmosphere, in Outer Space and Under Water (PTBT), the United States, the Soviet Union and the United Kingdom have conducted their testing at underground sites. France continued to carry out atmospheric tests on French territory in the South Pacific (see sect. F below) till 1974 when it changed to underground testing only. China ended atmospheric testing in Sinkiang in 1980.[4]

The nuclear-weapon States have based their decisions to develop new nuclear weapons, upgrade and test new nuclear-weapon systems on the following grounds: to ensure effectiveness of the nuclear deterrent by continued modernization of the nuclear stockpile; to maintain the reliability, survivability and safety of nuclear stockpiles; to allow the nuclear Powers to subject command and control equipment to nuclear effects; to permit development of smaller warheads with potentially limited collateral effects.[5]

The nuclear-weapon States have used testing to amass a vast amount of weapons expertise and a wide range of nuclear weapons. They feel that nuclear weapons must be tested if they are to remain credible. While some nuclear explosions have been used to test trigger and safety mechanisms, many nuclear warhead components can be tested without an explosion.

C.
Costs of acquiring and maintaining nuclear weapons

Both of the two previous United Nations studies on nuclear weapons (1968 and 1980) tried to estimate the costs associated with the acquisition of nuclear weapons by a State that decides on such an undertaking. The two studies agreed that a nuclear weapons programme would cost less in real terms to implement at their respective times of preparation than it did in 1945. This was attributed to technological progress in several fields, in conjunction with a wide dissemination of related knowledge within the framework of peaceful nuclear energy development. However, the two studies also agreed that any nuclear weapons programme would still be very expensive. The establishment and operation of a nuclear reactor or an enrichment plant or both would be very costly. The development of an advanced, dedicated delivery system might cost even more.

The costs of a nuclear reactor may be subdivided into three main categories: the cost of constructing the reactor, the fuel costs and the operational and maintenance costs. The cost of construction depends on the capacity, size, location, design and type of reactor to be built as well as on the availability of a skilled work force. Therefore, the investment cost for capital equipment is highly variable from reactor to reactor. The cost of fuel is more predictable, depending only upon price and quantity. Operational and maintenance costs also vary with the size and type of operation, although these costs are more stable from year to year.

The cost to a country of trying to develop and construct nuclear weapons and their delivery systems would be enormous and a call on the national budget that only a relatively small number of countries could sustain. Not only would a country have to divert a significant quantity of its human, technological and material resources to the project, but it would also have to devote its highest quality resources to this task. The infrastructure required to support a peaceful nuclear power programme is extensive; the demands of a nuclear weapons programme go well beyond that, particularly if the country has to develop an indigenous enrichment capacity to provide fissile materials for the weapons. Added to these already huge costs would be the expense of developing advanced dedicated delivery systems.

It is easier to construct and operate a dedicated plutonium production reactor than an electrical-power-producing reactor. Investment costs for the simplest type of graphite-moderated reactor giving enough plutonium-239 for two weapons annually (10 kg of plutonium) are estimated to be in the range of $25 to $50 million. The capital cost of a reprocessing plant to extract plutonium from irradiated fuel would amount to an additional $50 million. Personnel requirements for construction and operation are modest and plutonium could be produced four years after the start of the construction. In order to obtain plutonium for 10 to 20 weapons per year with a safe and reliable reactor, investment costs would range up to perhaps $1,000 million and the project would require some 50 to 75 engineers and 150 to 200 skilled technicians. The time span until the first output of plutonium would be five to seven years.[6]

For an enrichment plant, costs may be categorized as for a reactor. The operational and maintenance costs are often proportional to the separation work actually done, which is indicative of the size and activity of the operation. This is often measured in mass separative work units (kg SWU) per time unit. The amount of separative work needed to produce a given quantity of enriched uranium depends on the type of plant, the quality of the "feed", i.e. the input, the level of enrichment of the final product and the residual U-235 content of the depleted "tails". For instance, to produce, in a certain plant, one kilogram of reactor fuel, enriched to 3 per cent from natural uranium with a 0.2 per cent uranium-235 content in the tails, 4.25 kg SWU is needed. To produce the same amount of weapon-grade material under the same conditions requires 226 kg SWU.[7]

Though costs can vary widely, all enrichment plants are expensive. In the United States, by the end of 1984, the total investment in plant and capital equipment for all three United States gaseous diffusion plants was $3.86 billion (an average of $1.28 billion each). According to unofficial sources, at the end of 1986, 2.59 million kg SWU went for United States defence activities, at the price of approximately $82–$100 per kg SWU.[8]

Some academic sources estimate that the total amount world wide of weapon-grade uranium produced since the Second World War ranges between 1,000 and 2,000 tons. Similarly, the total quantity of weapon-grade plutonium produced world wide amounts to 100-200 tons.

Currently, the United States is no longer producing enriched uranium for its nuclear weapons, since it has sufficient resources in its stockpile and in old weapons that it plans to scrap in the near future.

D.
Peaceful uses of nuclear explosive devices

Since the advent of the nuclear age in 1945, the international community has sought both to use nuclear energy for peaceful purposes and at the same time to prevent the spread of nuclear weapons. The issue of peaceful nuclear explosions (PNEs) is closely connected with the pursuit of these two goals. While nuclear explosions have a potential of being carried out for civil purposes, the practical technical and economic benefits of such use of a nuclear device remain in doubt.

Moreover, the prevalent view is that the technology for developing any explosive nuclear device is not distinguishable from that involved in the development of a nuclear weapon and that the explosion of such a device for peaceful purposes is indistinguishable from a nuclear-weapon test. A non-nuclear-weapon State capable of exploding a nuclear device could therefore emerge as a nuclear-weapon State in a significantly shorter time.[9]

Two broad categories of potential peaceful use of nuclear explosive devices have been identified: (a) excavation and landscaping (e.g. canal and dam construction) and (b) contained application (e.g. curbing runaway gas well fires, stimulating oil and gas production, creating storage cavities and conducting deep seismic soundings). Soviet peaceful nuclear explosions have encompassed all of the uses described above.[10]

The United States and the Soviet Union, hopeful of achieving technical success and economic advantages from peaceful nuclear explosions, each began conducting PNE-related test explosions in the 1960s. France carried out research on peaceful nuclear explosions but did not conduct any tests. China and the United Kingdom have never expressed any interest in peaceful nuclear explosions, and there are no indications that they have ever had such programmes. In 1974 India announced that it had carried out a peaceful nuclear explosion; it is the only non-nuclear-weapon State to have done so. This event aroused concern among other countries.[11]

The United States peaceful nuclear explosions programme, established in 1957, consisted of an active research and development effort and 12 actual nuclear field tests to investigate possible uses for gas stimulation and large-scale excavation. The advantages of using nuclear explosions for these purposes were not demonstrated by the programme. Because of this and the increasing public concern for the environment and possible increases in radioactivity, the United States terminated its programme in 1977.[12]

The first explosives used in the United States peaceful nuclear explosions programme were existing nuclear weapons modified to meet underground emplacement conditions. As experimental data became available, however, it became clear that the United States peaceful nuclear explosion devices would require special characteristics to minimize health and safety effects; these characteristics would

include low-fission explosives for excavation and all-fission devices
to minimize residual tritium for use in oil and gas stimulation. All testing of the devices was done at national test sites, while the analysis of
each event focused on whether the device performed as expected and
what radioactive elements were present.[13]

The Soviet Union also had an active peaceful nuclear explosions
programme, conducting over 100 detonations since 1965. However,
the programme has been seriously scaled back. Excavation applications apparently were abandoned a decade ago, owing to discouraging
experimental results and strong public objections on environmental
grounds. The main Soviet efforts now seem to focus on creating underground facilities for storage of gas condensate and conducting deep
seismic soundings.[14]

Five major treaties on arms limitation and disarmament deal in
whole or in part with the issue of peaceful nuclear explosions, all at-
testing to the similarity of nuclear explosive devices for military and
for peaceful purposes (see chap. VIII).

The original optimism on the possible benefits of the PNE technology has now been reversed. The combination of environmental
problems, delicate arms control issues, cost and security and safety
problems have all contributed to a common understanding that the
PNE technology is generally impractical.

E.
Physical, medical and environmental effects of nuclear weapons production

The complete nuclear-weapons production cycle comprises
many operations, i.e. mining and milling of uranium, uranium enrichment, reactor fuel fabrication, operation of reactors for plutonium
production, spent fuel reprocessing, weapons manufacture, handling
of weapons, dismantling of weapons and final disposal of waste. Many
of these operations are also common to civilian use of nuclear energy.
Most, if not all of them, are associated with possible risks to the personnel involved and to the environment. Accidental releases of radioactive substances and chemicals during ongoing processes or by efflu-
ents, transports and so on resulting from mismanagement of wastes
may cause environmental damage.

The United States nuclear warhead production industry currently
consists of 17 major facilities in 13 states.[15]

There has been increased scrutiny by the United States of its nuclear reactors used to produce materials for nuclear weapons, reveal-
ing safety concerns at a number of the United States nuclear-material-
production facilities. Therefore, all of the United States Department
of Energy's nuclear-weapons-material-producing reactors have been
shut down as at early 1990. As a result, the United States has not
produced any new tritium since at least June 1988, as the Department's three operational tritium production reactors at the Savannah
River facility, in the state of South Carolina, have all been shut
down.

The United States is estimated to have about 500 metric tons of
weapon-grade uranium, enough to support all existing United States
nuclear weapons.[16] In 1964, President Lyndon Johnson decided that
the United States stockpile of highly enriched uranium was sufficient
to support American nuclear weapons requirements. Since then the
United States has not produced any additional highly enriched
uranium for weapons.[17]

The United States currently has about 100 metric tons of plutonium, enough to support its current stockpile of nuclear weapons.[18]
In addition to the plutonium in existing nuclear warheads, the United
States has reserve and scrap plutonium that could, depending on modernization requirements and retirements, continue to support a nuclear
arsenal for some time.[19] United States legislation prohibits diversion
of plutonium from civilian power plants to weapons use.

The Soviet Union is thought to have built a total of 14 military
nuclear reactors, the same number that the United States originally
built. Four of them have been closed down. The 10 Soviet reactors
that are still in service will soon have been operating for about the
same length of time as United States military reactors, before the
United States reactors were shut down.[20]

The Soviet Union has announced that in 1989 it stopped production of enriched uranium, that it closed in 1987 one reactor that was
producing weapon-grade plutonium and that it plans to close down
in 1989–1990 a few more such reactors. In 1989, the Soviet Union
announced that it planned to decommission by the year 2000 all
plutonium-producing reactors. Four reactors producing weapon-
grade plutonium in the vicinity of Kyshtym will be shut down by the
end of 1990. Out of six plutonium-producing reactors that will still be

operating, three reactors will be closed by 1996 and the last three before the year 2000.[21]

The Soviet Union has also been experiencing difficulties with its
nuclear-weapons production facilities. It has been reported that the
Kyshtym Industrial Complex, established in 1946 and therefore the
oldest nuclear-weapons production facility in the Soviet Union, was
experiencing difficulties similar to those of its American counterparts.
The plant has experienced severe radioactive and toxic pollution, critical mechanical lapses and public fears about health threats. This is
not a new problem for the Soviet Union. Mismanagement of nuclear
waste caused a huge explosion there in 1957 that showered hundreds
of square miles with dangerous radioactive particles. It forced the
evacuation of more than 10,000 people and created a radioactive zone
65 miles long and almost 6 miles wide. In addition, the Soviet Union
poured caesium, strontium and other nuclear wastes directly into a
lake within the complex, making it unfit for human use. More than 30
years later water reserves in the surrounding area are still undrinkable.[22]

The 1957 accident at Kyshtym, which was described in detail by
the Soviet press 32 years later, coupled with the accident at Chernobyl
in April 1986, has also caused popular anxiety in the Soviet Union
about nuclear technology. As a result of various incidents, both in the
Soviet Union and in the United States, domestic concerns about the
dangers people face from the weapons industry have begun to enter
the debate about the safety of nuclear facilities.[23]

These concerns have prompted the United States Department of
Energy to propose spending $28.6 billion over the next five years to
correct the conditions at civil and military nuclear sites around the
United States. The money would be used to clean up pollution, to
repair equipment and for research to develop new methods to dispose
of radioactive and chemical waste. The plan is intended to correct nuclear and chemical contamination and repair damage at 94 nuclear sites
in 19 states in the United States, of which 72 are no longer active.[24]

Under the plan, at least $13 billion is to be spent on the disposal
of low- and high-level radioactive wastes. The low-level waste includes cardboard boxes, gloves and other material contaminated with
radioactive substances, which are not acutely harmful but can be
dangerous with long-term exposure. The high-level waste consists of
radioactive elements like caesium and strontium. Most of these wastes

are stored as liquids. They emit penetrating radiation that can be lethal near the storage vessels even after very short exposure.[25]

Among the problems identified at United States nuclear-weapon production plants were:

a.   releases of radio-nuclides and other harmful substances into the air, water and soil;

b.   plants run without adequate worker protection or safety precautions;

c.   toxic and radioactive waste accumulating in thousands of dump sites; and

d.   hazardous materials being unsafely transported through heavily populated sections of major American cities.[26]

There is little information as to whether the other three nuclear-weapon States are having any problems with their military reactors on a scale similar to those being experienced by the United States and the Soviet Union. However, the United Kingdom has experienced some contamination, on at least one occasion, from a reactor used for production of weapon-grade fissile material. France has not met with any similar difficulties, according to French officials.

F.
Physical, medical and environmental effects of testing

Radioactive materials from atmospheric testing occasionally caused strong local contamination and were also distributed globally. However, since the signing of the PTBT, the United Kingdom, the Soviet Union and the United States have not conducted atmospheric tests.

Continued testing throughout the 1950s spread radioactive substances over Utah and Nevada and over ships and islands in the Pacific near the Bikini Atoll tests. Army troops were also placed near the atomic test sites in 1952 and 1953 as part of an exercise to test the effects of the use of nuclear weapons on combat readiness.[27] A higher incidence of cancer has been reported in these troops, although an explicit link to the tests has not been established. The concern about this global contamination led the United Nations to establish in 1955 the United Nations Scientific Committee on the Effects of Atomic Radiation (UNSCEAR). This Committee has reported to the General

Assembly on a regular basis on the levels of contamination and the associated health effects.

Fall-out has affected test areas, some of which have not yet been restored to safe, habitable conditions. Different components in the fall-out from a nuclear test remain radioactive for periods varying from a few days to many millennia. Despite precautions being taken, weather conditions occasionally led to significant amounts of radioactive material being carried to nearby inhabited regions. Some biological effects of the testing have been clearly demonstrated, such as the thyroid tumours following exposure after atmospheric tests of children on the Marshall Islands. Other alleged effects of exposure on, for example, troops from the United States and the United Kingdom, and on the population in the contaminated areas in the vicinity of the test sites are still being studied.

The effects of underground testing depend on the yield and depth of the blast as well as the geological character of the test site. The bulk of the radioactive debris is trapped within vitrified rock, which is formed in the explosion chamber during the test. Immediate releases of radioactive substances can occur by the venting of gas to the surface through the shattered rock above the chamber. While it is normal for rigorous safety precautions to be in force at underground test sites, instances of venting, of varying seriousness, have occurred. The health of test site workers, who work in close proximity to a range of radiation hazards, is closely monitored.[28]

For testing to be safe in the longer term, rock formations at test sites must be sound enough to prevent the leakage of high-grade radioactive material into the ground water over several thousand years. Critical factors include the leachability of the radioactive waste, the flow rate of the ground water, the absorption character of surrounding rock and the isolation of the site itself.[29] Scientific studies have reached various conclusions on the likelihood and severity of future leakages. However, there is a natural and widespread concern that test sites may not prove able to contain radioactive waste and that serious leaks could have environmental and medical consequences.

Underground nuclear tests also produce geological disturbances. The underground cavity formed by the explosion soon collapses, causing some surface disturbance. Seismic waves from the blast may affect the whole test site, adding to concerns about its long-term integrity and causing other damage in some cases, such as marine land-slides. Small seismic waves can be detected from great distances. However, underground nuclear tests are not thought to trigger larger earthquakes.

There are two test sites in the Soviet Union for the conduct of nuclear tests — one near the town of Semipalatinsk (Kazakhstan) and one on the island of Novaya Zemlya, between the Barents Sea and the Kara Sea in the Arctic Ocean. The first Soviet atomic bomb was exploded at the Semipalatinsk site in 1949 and in 1953 a hydrogen bomb was exploded there. Prior to 1963, atmospheric nuclear tests were carried out at that site.

In 1989, two commissions of experts were established at the request of public organizations in Kazakhstan, and they have brought to light a number of factors reflecting the adverse effect of tests on the population and on plant and animal life in areas of Kazakhstan adjacent to the test site. In particular, it has been determined that during the 14-year period when atmospheric tests were conducted, approximately 10,000 people were exposed to radiation in areas immediately adjacent to the test site. Among these 10,000, the average equivalent dose varied from 0.02 to 1.6 sievert (Sv). The remaining population received less than 0.02 Sv.[30] (As a comparison, for a professional who has to deal with ionizing radiation, an equivalent dose of up to 0.05 Sv over a year is not considered to be a health hazard, according to current international standards.)

Between 1959 and 1987 the mortality rate from leukaemia tripled in the Semipalatinsk region. Birth defects resulted in a significant increase in infant mortality. The incidence of births of children with subsequent mental retardation was three to five times higher in the areas adjacent to the test site than in the country as a whole. In a sample survey of the population conducted in 1989, almost half those examined showed decreased immunological resistance. As early as 1962, a medical commission of the Academy of Sciences of the Kazakh SSR established that the incidence of malignant tumours in the Semipalatinsk region was 35 per cent higher than average for the Republic.[31]

Following the conversion of the Semipalatinsk test site to use solely for underground tests, the radiation situation improved significantly. The level of background radiation is now almost the same as natural background radiation. Nevertheless, after each underground nuclear explosion, water is lost from the wells and water supply and sewage pipes burst. Cracks appear in the walls of buildings. Even today, unusually large numbers of people are treated in polyclinics and both children and teachers show a sharply reduced ability to work.

The United States test area is situated in Nevada. Early United States nuclear tests had been carried out in New Mexico, Mississippi, Colorado, in the central Pacific on atolls in the Marshall Islands, the Northern Line Islands and in the Aleutian Islands. The Nevada test site was chosen as a continental proving ground in December 1950 to reduce the expense and logistic problems of testing in the Pacific.

The Nevada test site has been used for both atmospheric and underground testing. It has been reported that in the 1950s and 1960s employees at the site had been exposed to dangerous levels of radiation during post-explosion work. The Office of Technological Assessment has also disclosed that 126 underground tests since 1970 have released roughly 54,000 curies of radiation, which is only a very small release compared with that emanating from an atmospheric explosion. The Office has concluded that these releases from underground tests have not jeopardized the health of nearby residents.

The United Kingdom uses the Nevada test site for its underground tests. Early United Kingdom tests had been carried out in the central Pacific and in Australia.

There is little information available about the conditions at the Chinese test site at Lop Nor in Singkiang. The testing base covers an area of more than 100,000 km^2 in the Gobi desert. Both atmospheric and underground tests have been conducted there.

Nuclear testing in the South Pacific has become an area of contention between some of the nuclear-weapon States and a number of South Pacific States.

French nuclear testing takes place on the atolls of Mururoa and Fangataufa in the territory of French Polynesia. France began atmospheric testing there in 1966, switching to underground testing alone in 1974. Recently, France announced that its test programme would be reduced from eight to six tests annually and the level of secrecy surrounding the programme would be reduced.

There has been a long international debate about the safety and desirability of French tests. France says that testing is necessary to ensure the effectiveness of its nuclear forces. It is satisfied that the testing programme is safe. The test sites are isolated (1,500 people live in a 500 km radius) and a variety of safety precautions have been taken.

French nuclear testing is a matter of concern to most South Pacific countries. They strongly object to manifestations of nuclear weaponry in the South Pacific, a sentiment reflected in the Treaty of Rarotonga (see chap. VII), and have made many calls for France to stop testing in the region. In 1973, upon the request of Australia and New Zealand, the International Court of Justice indicated that the Government of France should avoid nuclear tests causing the deposit of radioactive fall-out on the territory of Australia, New Zealand, the Cook Islands, Niue or the Tokelau Islands. However, in 1974 the Court found that France had entered into a commitment not to carry out atmospheric tests in the South Pacific and that, accordingly, the Australian and New Zealand claims no longer had any object.[32] Concerns continue to be expressed about the environmental and health effects of French underground testing. In particular, some scientists feel there is a significant risk of radioactivity leaking into the surrounding ocean over time.[33] However, France has allowed several independent studies which have shown no significant radioactive pollution of the areas investigated.[34]

Notes   1.   NPT/CONF.III/64/I.
         2.   *Effects of a Comprehensive Test Ban Treaty on United States National Security Interests*, hearings before the Panel on the Strategic Arms Limitation Talks and the Comprehensive Test Ban Treaty of the Intelligence and Military Application of Nuclear Energy Subcommittee of the Committee on Armed Services, House of Representatives, 95th Congress, second session, August 1978. See also *Announced United States Nuclear Tests, July 1945–December 1984*, Department of Energy, 1985; Thomas B. Cochran *et al.*, eds. *Nuclear Weapons Databook, Vol. II: United States Nuclear Warhead Production*, Cambridge, Mass., Ballinger, 1987, pp. 44–47 and pp. 151–178; *Test Ban Issues: Hearing of the Committee on Foreign Relations*, United States Senate, 100th Congress (second session, 6 October 1988, Washington, US Government Printing Office, 1989; and *Nuclear Weapons and Security: The Effects of Alternative Test Ban Treaties: Report*, United States House of Representatives, Committee on Foreign Affairs, 101st Congress, first session, June 1989, Washington, US Government Printing Office, 1989.
         3.   "Nuclear notebook", *Bulletin of the Atomic Scientists*, vol. 46, No. 3 (April 1990), p. 57; see also Ragnhild Ferm, "Nuclear explosions", in *SIPRI Yearbook 1990*, New York, Oxford University Press, 1990, pp. 56 and 57 (table 2.A.4).

4. In the course of undergound nuclear testing, a shaft is drilled in suitable rock formations to a depth of 200–1,500 metres. A canister containing the nuclear device and equipment to monitor the blast is placed in it, and cables are run down the shaft to transmit data to the surface. The shaft is then plugged with debris and sealing agents to prevent the release of radioactive gases. Data is received as the charge is detonated and small samples may be taken from the rock structure after the blast. In "weapon effects" tests the procedure is rather different, involving the construction of large, accessible underground caverns to hold equipment, with barriers to shield the equipment from the blast. See footnote 3. See also Ragnhild Ferm, "Nuclear explosions", in *SIPRI Yearbook 1987*, p. 46. On the mechanics of underground testing, see Cochran, *et al.*, *op. cit.*, pp. 44–47.

5. See Steven Fetter, *Toward a Comprehensive Test Ban*, Cambridge, Mass., Ballinger, 1988, chap. 2, pp. 33-68.

6. Cost estimates in this paragraph are those given in the 1980 United Nations nuclear-weapons study, adjusted to current United States dollar value. The estimates do not reflect the fact that inflation has been more rapid in many other States, nor the existence of other factors that may influence costs.

7. Allan S. Krass, Peter Boskma, Boelie Elzen and Wim A. Smit, *Uranium Enrichment and Nuclear Weapon Proliferation*, London, Taylor and Francis Ltd., 1983, chap. 5, pp. 93–119; Cochran *et al.*, *op. cit.*, pp. 125–135.

8. Cochran *et al.*, vol. III, pp. 130 and 131.

9. See *Effects of a Comprehensive Test Ban Treaty on United States National Security Interests Hearings*, p. 57.

10. For a detailed discussion of PNEs, see Iris Y. P. Borg, "Nuclear explosions for peaceful purposes", in Jozef Goldblat and David Cox, eds., *Nuclear Weapons Tests: Prohibition or Limitation?*, New York, Oxford University Press, 1988, pp. 59–74; see also Ragnhild Ferm, "Nuclear explosions", *SIPRI Yearbook 1988*, p. 66.

11. See Bhupendra Jasani, "Introduction to Part IV", in *SIPRI*, eds., *Nuclear Energy and Nuclear Weapon Proliferation*, London, Taylor and Francis Ltd., 1979, pp. 288 and 289; and D. Davies, "Peaceful applications of nuclear explosions", in the same volume, pp. 300 and 301.

12. Borg, *op. cit.*, pp. 59–67.

13. *Ibid.*, pp. 60 and 61.

14. *Ibid.*, pp. 67–69.

15. Cochran, *et al.*, *op. cit.*, p. 26.

16. Cochran, *et al.*, *op. cit.*, pp. 5, 75, 83 and 191.

17. *Ibid.*, pp. 5, 82 and 85.

18. *Ibid.*, p. 75, as at end of fiscal year 1984.

19. *Ibid.*, pp. 74–78. With the completion of the INF Treaty and the likelihood of a START Treaty in the future, sufficient plutonium will be available from the warheads on missiles earmarked for dismantling for future modernization.

20. Center for Defense Information, *The Defense Monitor*, vol. 18, No. 4, 1989.

21. *Official Records of the General Assembly, Forty-fourth Session, Plenary Meetings*, 6th meeting.

22. See James E. Oberg, *Uncovering Soviet Disasters: Exploring the Limits of Glasnost*, New York, Random House, 1988, chap. 13, "The Urals disaster", pp. 211–228. See also John May, *The Greenpeace Book of the Nuclear Age*, New York, Pantheon, 1989, pp. 119–123 and 348.

23. *Sources, Effects and Risks of Ionizing Radiation*, United Nations Scientific Committee on the Effects of Atomic Radiation, 1988 report (United Nations publication, Sales No. E.88.IX.7).

24. See Philip Shenon, "Atomic cleanup is seen costing $92 billion", in *The New York Times*, 5 January 1989, p. A16; Keith Schneider, "US plans study of weapons plants' effects on public", in *The New York Times*, 13 January 1990, p. A6; and Keith Schneider, "Cost of cleanup at nuclear sites is raised by 50%", in *The New York Times*, 4 July 1990, p. A1. A detailed Department of Energy five-year plan for site clean-up and waste management was prepared in November 1989.

25. United States Department of Energy five-year plan, 1989.

26. Todd Perry, David Lewis and Janna Rolland, "The US nuclear weapons production complex: a public health and safety emergency", in *PSR Monitor*, vol. 5, No. 1, January 1989, p. 2.

27. Robert C. Williams and Philip L. Cantelon, eds., *The American Atom*, Philadelphia, University of Pennsylvania, 1984, pp. 177 and 178.

28. See A. C. McEwan, "Environmental effects of underground nuclear explosions", chap. 4 in Goldblat and Cox, *op. cit.*, pp. 75-91.

29. *Ibid.*

30. *Pravda*, 12 February 1990. On the Kazakhstan public organizations that have requested inquiries into testing dangers, see Michael R. Gordon, "Soviets cut back nuclear testing as hazards become a local issue", in *The New York Times*, 8 July 1989, p. A3; and Paul Quinn-Judge, "Activists mute Soviet nuclear tests", in *The Christian Science Monitor*, 12 April 1989, pp. 1 and 2.

31. *Pravda*, 6 April 1990.

32. *Nuclear Tests (Australia v. France), Interim Protection, Order of 22 June 1973, I.C.J. Reports 1973*, p. 99; *Nuclear Tests (New Zealand v. France) Interim Protection, Order of 22 June 1973, I.C.J. Reports 1973*, p. 135; *Nuclear Tests (Australia v. France), Judgment of 20 December 1974, I.C.J. Reports 1974*, p. 253, *Nuclear Tests (New Zealand v. France) Judgment of 20 December 1974, I.C.J. Reports 1974*, p. 457.

33. Manfred P. Hochstein and Michael J. O'Sullivan, "The underground hydrology of Mururoa Atoll" in *New Zealand Engineering*, Wellington, 1 October 1986, pp. 47–49.

34. H. R. Atkinson, P. J. Davies, D. R. Davy, L. Hill and A. C. McEwan, *Report of a New Zealand, Australian and Papua New Guinea Scientific Mission to Mururoa Atoll*, Wellington, New Zealand Ministry of Foreign Affairs, 1984, pp. 10–12; Fondation Cousteau, *Mission scientifique de la Calypso sur le site d'expérimentations nucléaires de Mururoa*, Paris, Fondation Cousteau, 1988, pp. 49–52.

VI
Effects of use of nuclear weapons and consequences of nuclear war

A.
General

The existing knowledge of the effects of the use of nuclear weapons is far from complete. In only two instances were nuclear weapons used in actual war conditions, against the Japanese cities of Hiroshima and Nagasaki in 1945. The outcome of these explosions has been painstakingly investigated, yet considerably different data are given by different sources, in particular with regard to the number of casualties. Even in recent years, new findings have been brought to light about the detailed effects of the bombings of Japan.

The studies on the effects of a nuclear war are generally based on data from Hiroshima and Nagasaki, nuclear-weapon testing and extrapolations or scientific hypotheses that by definition cannot be verified. Irrespective of the sophistication of the various models applied in the different studies, it should be borne in mind that no desk calculations could give a true picture of the consequences of nuclear warfare. The accounts given below should therefore be considered only as indications of the magnitude of the effects of nuclear war as described in these studies.

Studies carried out to determine the effects of the use of nuclear weapons have all used different war scenarios and applied various other assumptions. The scenarios ranged from the explosion of one nuclear weapon to an all-out nuclear exchange. Apart from the number of weapons used, other scenario parameters are, for instance, the explosive yield and height of burst of the individual weapons, the character of their targets, especially the population density in the target area, and climate and weather conditions. The results have usually been presented as estimates of the number of people killed and injured, as well as of material damage to built-up areas, loss of industrial capacity, and so forth.

Should large numbers of nuclear weapons ever be used, the total effect would be much larger and more complex than the sum of individual cases. Immediate damage may be enhanced by interactions of a direct and physical nature. Important additional uncertainties pertain to the overall social, economic and political aftermath of the sudden and widespread devastation that a nuclear war would entail. There are also long-term, large-scale physical consequences, including climatic effects, of a war involving many nuclear explosions. All of these large-scale consequences will affect non-combatant nations, partially on a global scale, for a long time after the war.

B.
Effects of one nuclear explosion

The explosion of a nuclear weapon causes damage in several ways: intense thermal radiation, a powerful blast wave and nuclear radiation from the fireball and from radioactive fall-out. There is also a pulse of electromagnetic radiation harmful to electrical systems. Of these, the fall-out has a delayed effect, while all the others are immediate.[1]

When a nuclear weapon is exploded above ground, the first notice-able effect is a blinding flash of intense white light. The light is emitted from the surface of the "fireball", a roughly spherical mass of very hot air (the temperature is of the order of 10 million C) and weapon resi-dues, which develops quickly around the exploding weapon and con-tinues to grow until it reaches a maximum radius, which depends on the yield.[2] During this time, and for some time after, the fireball emits thermal radiation both as light and — mainly — heat. When the fireball rises, it cools off and is gradually transformed into a huge mushroom-shaped cloud. A column of dust and smoke sucked up from the ground forms the stem of the mushroom. After some 10 minutes, when the cloud is fully developed, it will have a height and a diameter of several kilometres, dependent on the yield. By then, about one third of the explosive energy has been released as heat.[3]

Thermal radiation

The effects of thermal radiation would be manifold. Within and close to the fireball, everything would be vaporized or melt. The thermal radiation could be expected to kill or severely injure people directly exposed to it at relatively large distances. Materials that are easily ignited, such as thin fabrics, paper or dry leaves, may catch fire at even longer distances. This may cause numerous additional fires, which under some conditions may form a huge fire storm enveloping much of the target area and adding numerous further casualties. That was the case in Hiroshima, although it is considered less likely in modern cities.[4]

Air blast

The blast wave carries about half the explosive energy and travels much slower than the various forms of radiation, but always at supersonic speed. The arrival of the blast wave is experienced as a sudden and shattering blow, immediately followed by a hurricane-force wind directed outwards from the explosion. Near the explosion, virtually all buildings would be utterly demolished and people inside them killed. At somewhat larger distances, ordinary buildings would be crushed or heavily damaged by the compressional load as they would be engulfed by the blast overpressure and the wind drag. People inside could be crushed under the weight of the falling build-ings, hurt by the flying debris of broken windows, furniture, etc., or even suffocated by the dense dust of crushed brick and mortar. All the primary blast destruction would take place during a few seconds.[5]

Some of the energy in the blast is transferred to the ground, creating a shock wave in the underlying soil or rock strong enough to damage even fortified underground structures. The transfer of energy would become more efficient the closer to ground level the explosion occurs.

Nuclear radiation

Before any visible phenomena occur, the exploding device starts to emit an intense burst of neutrons and gamma rays. Virtually all of this radiation is released during the first one or two seconds. It is rapidly attenuated with distance as it travels through the air. For an explosion similar to those over Hiroshima or Nagasaki, this radiation is strong enough to render human beings in the open unconscious within minutes at distances up to 700 or 800 m from ground-zero.[6] The exposed persons, if they survive the blast and heat, would die in less than one or two days from the radiation injury. The radiation re-ceived at a distance of 1,300–1,400 m from such an explosion would also be fatal but death may be delayed up to about a month. At 1,800 m or more from ground-zero few if any acute radiation injuries would be expected to occur. However, late radiation injuries may be induced by lower radiation levels. In addition, acute radiation sickness caused by non-lethal doses could trail off with a state of general weakness protracted over months and years.[7]

Electromagnetic pulse

Simultaneously, a small part of the gamma ray energy is converted to electromagnetic energy through interaction with the surrounding air and develops a strong electromagnetic field, which is also propagated outwards (see figure 1). This phenomenon, known as electromagnetic pulse (EMP), takes the form of a very short burst of electromagnetic waves in the radio frequency spectrum, up to at least 1 MHz, which trails off within about one thousandth of a second. Electronic equipment might suffer EMP damage even if it were not connected to any antennae.[8]

Nuclear fall-out

The fireball, and later the cloud, contains most of the radioactive atoms, mostly fission products, that were formed in the explosion. While the total weight of these fragments is small, about 1 kg, their combined activity one hour after the explosion equals that of several thousand tons of radium (although the emitted radiation is somewhat different). This activity decays rapidly, however; during the first two weeks it decreases to one thousandth of what it was one hour after the explosion. As the cloud develops, the radioactive atoms are incorporated in larger particles formed by condensing vapours and mixed-in dust and dirt. The range of the radiation is relatively short compared to either the height of the cloud base or the size of the devastated area. For this reason, the radioactive particles in the cloud do not constitute a health hazard until they are deposited on the ground as radioactive fall-out.[9]

The radioactive cloud drifts, changes shape and eventually disintegrates under the action of the winds at those altitudes where it is stabilized. At the same time, the particles carrying the activity subside with speeds that depend strongly on their size. In the case of an air burst, most particles will be very small and it may take from days to years for them to reach the ground. By that time they have lost most of their activity and have been scattered over a wide area. Fall-out over intermediate times may be denoted tropospheric, while the very

Figure 1.   *High-altitude electromagnetic pulse*

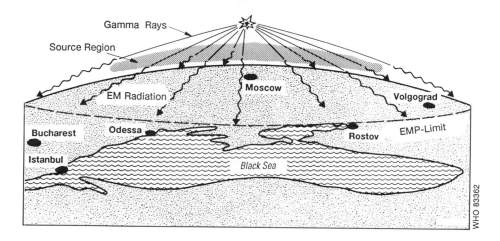

A nuclear explosion at, say, 100 km above the Earth will create EMP phenomena within a 1,200 km circle. If, for instance, Moscow were chosen as ground-zero, the EMP disturbance would reach from the Kola Peninsula to the Black Sea. It would also cover parts of Finland, Poland and Romania. (The heights of the burst and the source region are greatly exaggerated in comparison to the curvature of the Earth.)

slow deposition of particles injected into the stratosphere is usually referred to as global fall-out. This fall-out radiation does not cause any acute ill effects, but over the decades to follow it will contribute to the occurrence of "late effects" (additional cancers and genetic injuries).[10]

When the nuclear weapon explodes at or close to the ground, with the fireball in direct contact with the surface, thousands of tons of soil are injected into the hot vapours. Large (diameters up to one millimetre or more) particles then carry a significant part of the residual activity. These particles come down to earth in a matter of hours or even minutes and create an intensely radioactive contamination field in the downwind vicinity of ground-zero. This so-called immediate fall-out gives rise to acutely lethal radiation doses for unprotected people over large areas. The possibility of late radiation injuries in this area is also much larger than in the case of an air burst.[11]

The size of the areas affected by the various effects described above will depend primarily on the explosive yield and the height above the ground of the explosion. It is also influenced by other factors specific to each situation such as weather conditions. Some of these factors are not yet fully understood.[12] Wind velocity is particularly important for fall-out.

It is generally considered that the area on the ground affected immediately would be circular. Its size increases with increasing yield but in less than direct proportion to it. Roughly, ten-fold or hundred-fold increases in the yield produce five-fold and twenty-fold increases respectively in the area devastated by air blast.[13] The area exposed to a certain level of thermal radiation increases more rapidly with yield than does that affected by air blast. This implies that thermal effects — fires and burns — will become progressively more dominant with increasing weapon yields. Conversely, the initial nuclear radiation loses most of its importance when the yield increases.

Areas of damage caused by different effects will vary with the height of burst, generally decreasing somewhat with decreasing height. These variations are relatively unimportant in comparison to the most dramatic additional effect of explosions close to the ground surface, i.e. the generation of local radioactive fall-out, as described above. In a matter of hours, the fall-out will contaminate an area downwind of the explosion that is very large compared to that affected by blast and heat. The size of the contaminated area is expected to be roughly proportional to the fraction of the explosive yield due to fission, although the actual distribution of fall-out is determined by winds and precipitation.[14]

Another influence of variations in the height of burst relates to EMP. Surface or low air bursts will generate EMP that may have harmful effects on electrical and electronic equipment out to a distance of about 3–10 km from ground-zero, depending on the explosion yield and the equipment sensitivity. The strength of the EMP at the ground will then decrease with increasing height of burst up to an altitude of 10 to 15 km. When bursts occur at still higher altitudes, a strong EMP will again be experienced on the ground. This is due to the combined effects of atmospheric density variation in the altitude and the geomagnetic field. This EMP covers a wide area, since it extends outwards in all directions as far as the line of sight from the burst point. A nuclear explosion at an altitude of 80 km would affect a circular area with a radius of about 1,000 km. Thus a high altitude burst might cause EMP damage over entire countries while all other effects (except possibly flash blindness at night) would be negligible.[15]

C.
Levels of immediate destruction in various scenarios

1.

Effects of a nuclear explosion over cities

Many of the studies referred to above have described the immediate consequences of nuclear air bursts — often with high explosive yields — over large cities. The number of fatalities and level of destruction in such a scenario depend on many factors, including the size of the city and the distribution of its population in relation to weapon yield, the height of burst and ground-zero location.

That one nuclear weapon of relatively low yield can destroy a city of intermediate size and kill a large portion of its population was convincingly demonstrated in August 1945. The actual numbers of people killed or injured in Hiroshima and Nagasaki are still under debate. In the case of Hiroshima, between 310,000 and 320,000 people were exposed to the various effects of the atomic explosion. Of these, between 130,000 and 150,000 had died by December 1945 and an estimated 200,000 by 1950, if latent effects are included. In

Figure 2.   *A Hiroshima bomb over New York*

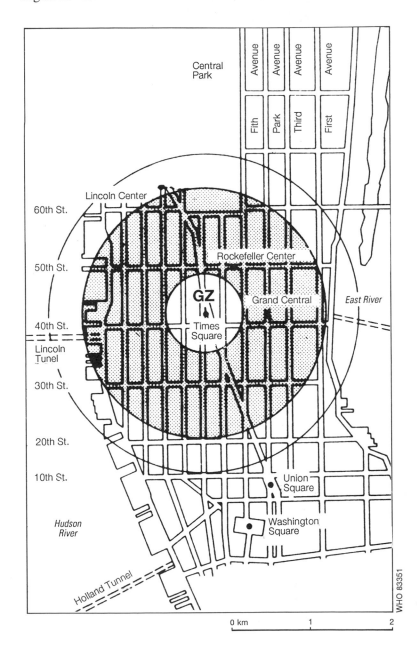

WHO 83351

Figure 3.   *A 15 Mt air burst over New York*

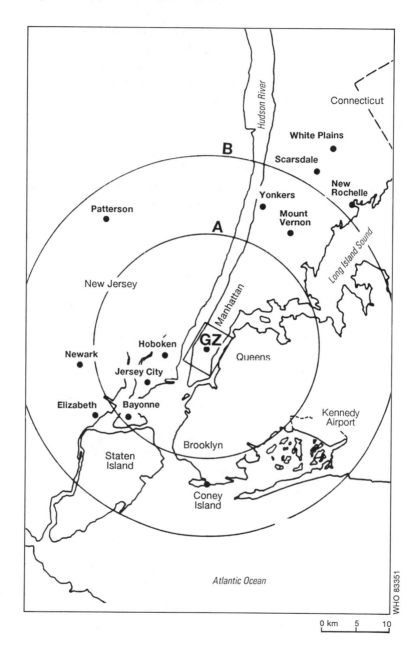

Nagasaki, the corresponding numbers are 270,000–280,000, 60,000–80,000 and 100,000.[16]

The 1980 United Nations study reported the consequences of a 100 kt low airburst over the centre of a European city with 0.5–1 million inhabitants. Scientists had estimated that such an explosion could kill up to half the population, that at least half of all buildings within a radius of 5–6 km would be destroyed by blast, and that roughly that same area might be ablaze with fires within an hour after the explosion.

Possible consequences of megaton explosions over large cities were summarized in the United Nations study in 1980 (see figures 2 and 3). The United States Congress Office of Technology Assessment (OTA) in 1979 and the World Health Organization (WHO) in 1984, as well as several independent organizations, have also dealt with the subject. Assuming only airbursts, which means disregarding the possibility of local fall-out with its associated additional casualties, the following table summarizes the results:

City	Weapon yield (Megatons)	Casualties (Millions)		Source
		Killed	Total	
Detroit	1	0.5	1.1	OTA 1979[17]
Leningrad	1	1.0	2.0	OTA 1979[18]
New York	15		5–10	United Nations 1980[19]
London	1	1.6	3.2	WHO 1987[20]

As another example, an independent study group at Princeton[21] estimated the casualties that would result if the 100 most populated regions in the United States and the Soviet Union were exposed to one 1 Mt airburst each. This was estimated to cause up to more than 70 million casualties, of which about 90 per cent would be killed outright, in the United States and even larger numbers in the Soviet Union. The resulting numbers may vary by a factor of up to 2, depending on what type of model is being used.

2.
Consequences of a nuclear exchange

Most studies of the possible consequences of a nuclear exchange assume that a multitude of nuclear weapons are employed. These studies have some general points in common: (a) in any densely populated area, the ratio of civilians to military among those killed and injured would be very high; and (b) if ground bursts occurred, the number of casualties would rise significantly, owing to radiation injuries, since adequate shelters would not be available. The higher the yields of the explosions at ground surface the more important fall-out becomes. The number of civilians killed or injured by fall-out could far outnumber those affected by blast and heat.

Several studies have considered the consequences of a nuclear war in which all the weapons used are "tactical", having yields from 1 kt to some 100 kt, and are aimed at military targets. In some European scenarios, the number of explosions has been taken to be more than 1,000, with a combined yield in the range of 20–100 Mt, and the number of early deaths among civilians has been estimated to be between 10 and 20 million.[22]

Many studies of a major nuclear exchange, involving large numbers of strategic warheads, have been carried out, particularly in the United States. In these studies various scenarios have been described, generally categorized as either counter-force or counter-value strikes.[23]

In a counter-force strike, surface bursts would probably be used in large numbers, as they maximize the probability of destroying hard military targets, e.g. ICBM silos. The major cause of civilian casualties would then be early fall-out. Attacks against strategic bomber bases and strategic submarine bases might use air bursts and, to the extent that these facilities were located close to population centres, blast and thermal effects would cause considerable damage in such areas.

The United States Congressional Office of Technology Assessment (OTA) study published in 1979 quotes United States government studies indicating that between 2 and 20 million Americans would be killed within 30 days after a counter-silo attack on the United States ICBM sites.[24] The same study concludes that a comprehensive counter-force attack on the United States would produce about 14 million dead even if the present fall-out shelter capability were utilized. A United States counter-force strike against the Soviet Union would result in somewhat similar numbers of casualties, according to OTA. The majority of fatalities within 30 days of a counter-force attack would be caused by radiation due to early fall-out from surface bursts.[25] Other studies are in approximate agreement with these results.

In the studies referred to above, extensive sheltering of the civilian population is assumed. An uninterrupted stay in shelter during several weeks would be required to avoid still larger casualties. This would cause serious problems of sanitation, food and water supply, air filtration, health, communication to the outer world, psychological tensions, and so on.

After a counter-force strike, economic activities, especially in contaminated areas, would be disrupted for months and perhaps years. Furthermore, radioactive fall-out would cause serious problems to agriculture. Livestock would have little protection against fall-out. A severe decline in the supply of meat and dairy products would therefore result after a certain period of time and many years would be required to build up new livestock. Radiation effects on crops would depend on the season, an attack in spring causing more damage than one in the summer or early autumn. Radioactive elements filtering down into the ground water would be taken up by plants and, through grazing, by cattle and other animals. Quantities of radioactive substances could then enter the human system through consumption of foodstuffs from contaminated areas and contribute to the total number of late radiation injuries (see sect. D below).

The national capacity for food production, processing and distribution would probably be even more severely affected by an extensive counter-value attack than by a counter-force strike. Destruction of storage facilities, processing plants and transport facilities would result in a general food shortage within a short period of time. The destruction of virtually all petroleum refinery capacity, pipeline systems, and so on would have immediate consequences for transportation, heating and electrical power production. A counter-value attack could well entail the successive decay, if not the complete collapse, of social and political institutions.

The task of the survivors after a large nuclear war would be beyond our comprehension and they could face the complete breakdown of international order. In these circumstances reconstruction might be all but impossible.

3.

Consequences of damaging nuclear installations

The possibility must be taken into account that nuclear power industry installations, such as nuclear reactors, reprocessing plants or storage for spent nuclear fuel and radioactive waste, might be hit by nuclear explosions. Should this happen, most or all of their radioactive content might be surged into the explosion and add to the fall-out from the explosion itself. If one or a few such installations were destroyed, the additional amount of radioactive substances released would be limited. If, however, such installations were systematically targeted, the additional amount of radioactive substances released would be very substantial.[26]

The production rate of radioactive substances in a 1,000 MW nuclear electrical generating station is equal to that of one 60 kt atomic bomb every day, but after some time of reactor operation most of the short-life radiation would be limited to their saturation levels and the long-life radiation would dominate. In reprocessing plants and waste storages, only long-life radioactivity would remain.[27] Because of this equilibrium, the activity released from a reactor would become gradually more important in comparison to that contained in the explosion debris as time goes by.

Systematic destruction of nuclear facilities would thus add marginally to the short-term radiation after the attacks, but after a week or so, the contribution from destroyed facilities to the radiation effects would dominate. In areas with many nuclear installations, like Europe, North America and Japan, destruction of these facilities would make large areas uninhabitable for a century or more.[28] Comparison could be made with the Chernobyl accident, where part of the radioactive content of one reactor was released without the driving force of a nuclear explosion.[29]

D.
Medical effects

During the 1980s, considerable attention was given to the study and description of the medical aspects of nuclear war. Generally speaking, injuries related to nuclear explosions fall into three groups — mechanical, thermal and radiation-induced — although all kinds of combinations are likely.[30] Psychological effects would be likely to add to social disruption in a nuclear exchange. Mechanical injuries (fractures, soft tissue wounds, crush injuries) as well as thermal injuries (burns), are well known to medical science in general. In a nuclear context, though, problems would arise from the huge numbers of casualties and lack of resources. Acute radiation injuries, on the other hand, are uncommon in peacetime. The symptoms are often unspecific, at least initially, rendering the diagnosis uncertain. No specific remedies exist. In addition, delayed effects of radiation are quite different from acute radiation illness.[31]

1.

Mechanical and thermal injuries

An explosion may cause mechanical injury by overpressure acting directly on the human body or by causing the person to be swept away or dragged by the blast wind and thrown against a hard surface. The number of casualties is likely to be much higher after a nuclear explosion over a built-up area as a result of heavier material destruction, such as collapsing building structures, flying debris, and so forth.

Thermal injuries are mainly skin burns caused by the heat radiation (flash burns) or by fires ignited by this radiation (flame burns). In addition, the flash of heat and light might cause injuries to the eyes. Internal burns from inhalation of hot air or gases may occur in areas on fire, as well as toxic effects or asphyxiation from smoke and fumes. Flash burns, which are typical of nuclear explosions, are generated within a fraction of a second, whereas flame burns develop more slowly. The damage to tissue is not quite the same, as internal organs are more affected by the slower heating in flame burns.[32]

Moderate burns over 20 per cent of the body, or severe burns over 10 per cent, are considered to be grave even under circumstances favourable to treatment and healing. If no treatment at all is available, mortality from burn injuries will be very high. For instance, a 40 per cent burn might be fatal in one case out of five if medical treatment is optimal, but fatal in all cases if treatment is delayed for 24 hours.[33]

2.

Radiation injuries

The most specific medical effects related to a nuclear explosion are the radiation injuries.[34] Ionizing radiation from such explosions would always inflict some damage to biological tissue. Therefore, humans, animals and plants would be affected. Generally speaking, the larger the radiation dose, the more severe the resulting radiation injury to the organism. The injury to the individual caused by any given dose, would vary, however, depending on the species, age and general condition of the irradiated individual, the composition of the dose and the rate of irradiation.

Human radiation injuries can be of different types: acute radiation sickness, long-term effects that comprise an increased probability of late cancer and genetic effects, and short-term effects such as injuries in the prenatal stage and decreased immunological resistance.

A nuclear explosion would cause radiation injuries in several ways. Almost all of the initial radiation dose would be received from high-intensity radiation released within seconds in the immediate vicinity of the burst. This would be followed by the radiation from fall-out. The fall-out radiation emanates from particles outside the body, emitting harmful beta and gamma rays (external radiation). Large doses associated with early fall-out will be followed by lower intensity radiation received over a long period of time — from hours up to days, if it is possible to leave the area, otherwise much longer. There is some difference in biological response, however: a slowly accumulated dose is generally considered less harmful than an equally large instantaneous dose, owing to recovery mechanisms. On the other hand, recovery mechanisms are overwhelmed in many cases of repeated exposure.

In addition to the external radiation, living tissue may be injured by radiation from radioactive substances in the fall-out that have entered the organism by breathing, eating and drinking. The radiation doses received from such internal sources are likely to be much smaller than early external doses from fall-out. On the other hand, internal doses might accumulate for long times in specific organs and may thus contribute significantly to late radiation injuries, in particular, cancers.

Some types of cells are more radio-sensitive than others, and consequently certain organs or functions are disturbed at lower dose levels than others. The stem cells in the bone marrow, which produce various types of blood cells, are highly radio-sensitive. Hence, the so-called bone-marrow syndrome, characterized by low levels of certain blood cells, including lymphocytes, dominates the radiation response of the human body at moderate dose levels. Before this syndrome appears, however, there are other, unspecific symptoms called "prodromal". The term "acute radiation sickness" covers the prodromal stage, the bone-marrow syndrome and the gastro-intestinal and neurovascular syndromes appearing at higher doses.[35]

For the reasons described above, an important form of treatment of radiation injuries would be to prevent or reverse infections by providing the patients with the cleanest possible environment, preferably in isolated wards, and by using antibiotics, antimycotics and blood transfusions. Resources of these kinds will most likely be scarce or unavailable in the aftermath of a nuclear war.

Those who survive an acute radiation injury stand a larger risk than others of contracting certain diseases, in particular various forms of cancer. These afflictions are called late radiation injuries, as they may remain latent for years or decades before manifesting themselves. Even if the radiation exposure was not large enough to cause a state of acute sickness, it would produce an increased risk of late cancer. Radiologists now estimate the cancer risk per unit dose to be about five times higher than previously thought. This means that 5 to 10 cases per man-sievert[36] are expected instead of 1 to 2 cases.

When the exposure is an essentially uniform, whole-body irradiation from an external source, the total risk mentioned above is the sum of specific risks for different types of cancer, among which leukaemia, lung cancer and possibly stomach cancer are the most common. Exposure to radiation from internal sources will add to the overall dose received by a particular organ. Certain radio-nuclides accumulate in some organs.[37]

Radiation at much lower dose levels seems to be harmful to the human foetus, especially during the first four months or so of gestation. An exposure *in utero* can give rise to malformations, mental retardation and increased susceptibility to serious diseases, including childhood cancers, in addition to an increased risk of pre-natal or neo-natal death.

Furthermore, it is known that radiation affects the gonads (ovaries and testicles) and that radiation-induced mutations may then appear in the reproductive cells. It has been suggested that the changes may be transmitted to live offspring, thereby constituting a genetic damage that could become manifest in that or future generations. However, it is very difficult to assess the precise relationships between radiation doses and genetic damage in humans. The data available is insufficient to demonstrate genetic damage among the offspring of Hiroshima and Nagasaki survivors, for instance.

The 1980 United Nations study assumed in a "worst case scenario" that the source of radiation would be global fall-out from 10,000 Mt total explosive yield. It quotes one consequence of this to be between 5 and 10 million excess fatalities from cancer over a period of about 40 years. The recent scientific findings, as adopted by UNSCEAR,[38] would indicate corresponding numbers of 25-50 million, with an additional number of non-lethal tumours (including thyroid cancer) totalling perhaps 10 million. The cases of hereditary ill health caused by radiation may number a million or so in the first two generations and several million over the indefinite future.

3.
Other health effects

There are other long-term factors that must be taken into account. The need for medical care would obviously be most acute during the first hours or days following a nuclear exchange. For instance, one nuclear explosion could produce tens of thousands of burn victims. In view of the fact that the United States has facilities to treat about 2,000 serious cases of burns and Western Europe about 1,500, it is clear that even peacetime resources would be quite inadequate to manage the casualties.[39] Moreover, peacetime resources will not be available, as the qualified medical services either would be destroyed by the nuclear explosions or, if they are intact, may be too remote from the scene to be efficiently used.[40]

Furthermore, it is likely that production of medical supplies would be severely disturbed if major cities were attacked. Shortages of antibiotics or vaccines, for instance, would affect the whole world. The same would most likely hold true for other products, such as pesticides and detergents, which are needed to maintain hygienic standards and to fight different vectors of epidemic diseases. The severe food shortages and starvation that would be likely to occur in the aftermath of a major nuclear war would add considerably to the detrimental effects on global health.[41]

E.
Environmental and other global effects

It has long been recognized in principle that certain consequences of a major nuclear exchange would not be possible to limit to the territories of nuclear-weapon States, or the territories of other nations being included in the nuclear exchange. This fact has become more widely accepted during the last few years, concomitant with new findings that add further dimensions to the projections of the global aftermath of such an exchange.

1.
Climatic effects

The question of climatic perturbations has been thoroughly studied in the last decade. The analyses done up to 1980 had focused largely on the possible changes in the climate due to the injection of dust into the atmosphere caused by nuclear explosions. The new analyses first carried out in 1982 took into account in their calculations an additional element, i.e. the effects of widespread fires that would be ignited by the nuclear explosions. The new estimates of the cooling effects, brought about by the absorption of sunlight in the clouds of smoke, were considered so dramatic that the term "nuclear winter" was coined to describe them.[42]

During the following years, a substantial amount of additional research was carried out to explore more thoroughly the possible atmospheric changes induced by different forms of nuclear warfare, as well as the biological consequences of such changes. The most comprehensive study carried out so far is that made by the Scientific Committee on Problems of the Environment (SCOPE), a committee organized by the International Council of Scientific Unions. The results of this and other studies were summarized in a recently published United Nations study, the most relevant parts of which read as follows:[43]

"The scientific evidence is now conclusive that a major nuclear war would entail the high risk of a global environmental disruption. The risk would be greatest if large cities and industrial centres in the northern hemisphere were to be targeted in the summer months. During the first month, solar energy reaching the surface in mid-latitudes of the northern hemisphere could be reduced by 80 per cent or more. This would result in a decrease of continental averaged temperatures in mid-latitudes of between 5 to 20 C below normal within two weeks after the injection of smoke during summer months. In central continental areas individual temperature decreases could be substantially greater. ... Recent work ... suggests that these effects might be compounded by a decrease in rainfall of as much as 80 per cent over land in temperate and tropical latitudes. The evidence assessed to date is persuasive that residual scientific uncertainties are unlikely to invalidate these general conclusions.

"Beyond one month, agricultural production and the survival of natural ecosystems would be threatened by a considerable reduction in sunlight, temperature depressions of several degrees below normal and suppression of precipitation and summer monsoons. In addition, these effects would be aggravated by chemical pollutants, an increase in ultraviolet radiation associated with depletion of ozone and the likely persistence of radioactive 'hotspots'.

"The sensitivity of agricultural systems and natural ecosystems to variations in temperature, precipitation and light leads to the conclusion that the widespread impact of a nuclear exchange on climate would constitute a severe threat to world food production."

The residual scientific uncertainties mentioned above pertain to virtually all steps in the physical processes involved. Some examples of these uncertainties are the amount and characteristics of combustible materials that will burn after a specified explosion, the amounts of smoke and soot produced by the combustion, the optical and other properties of the smoke particles and the altitude to which the smoke rises. In addition, mathematical models used to simulate dynamic processes in the atmosphere must always be simplifications. However, much of the original uncertainty has been resolved through experimental research since 1983. Concurrently, more sophisticated models for numerical analysis of atmospheric processes have been employed. It should be recalled, however, that the basic uncertainties associated with the war scenarios, such as choice of weapon yields, targets, and so on cannot be resolved by science.

2.
Ozone layer effects

In addition to global climatic effects, the use of nuclear weapons is expected to affect the ozone layer as well. The fireball from a nuclear explosion heats the air to temperatures where oxygen and nitrogen molecules dissociate. In the subsequent cooling, a number of different nitrogen oxides are formed. It is estimated that a 1 Mt explosion would produce 5,000 tons of such oxides. In a large nuclear exchange the quantities of nitrogen oxides injected into the upper atmosphere would be considerably higher. These oxides would then reach the ozone layer in the stratosphere and might, through chemical reactions, partially destroy it in a few months.[44]

The extent to which the release of a given quantity of nitrogen oxides would deplete the ozone layer is not entirely clear. It is believed, however, that some 50 per cent of the ozone column might be depleted in a major nuclear exchange taking place during the summer months. In winter conditions the percentage would be smaller (some calculate 10–20 per cent).

Irrespective of the percentage of ozone layer depletion, the depletion would produce a number of harmful effects. For instance, since ozone is an effective barrier to solar ultraviolet radiation, its depletion would result in an increase of this radiation at the surface of the Earth. Although the full biological implications of increased ultraviolet radiation to ecosystems at various latitudes are not known, skin cancer is related to large amounts of ultraviolet radiation. Plants and animals might also be affected. Ocean phytoplankton, the basis of the world food chain, has been shown to be particularly sensitive.

3.
Other effects

Other world-wide effects of a major nuclear exchange are difficult to examine and assess. However, the fact that today's world is characterized by a large, intricate and increasing international interdependence in all aspects of life strongly suggests that significant global economic and social disruptions would be an unavoidable consequence of such an exchange.

In the first place, all countries in the world, combatants as well as non-combatants, would suffer a drastic reduction of foreign trade. This would be due to factors such as a decrease in production volume both of essential commodities and raw materials, disruption of services and breakdown of the organization of world commerce and communications. The world food supply and production would also be imperilled by trade disruptions. It is also expected that climatic perturbations would have some impact on agriculture in any major war scenario.

The 1980 United Nations study on nuclear weapons gave an indication of the possible global food situation after a nuclear exchange, without considering additional climatic problems. The 1985 study by the Scientific Committee on Problems of the Environment,[45] however, provided more analysis of the vulnerability to losses of agricultural productivity and the potential for recovery of food production as well as various assumptions regarding the climatic disturbances. A simplified assessment was made for some 120 other countries. The results were, in brief, that very few countries had a capability to support their populations either in the short term, by using stored food, or in the longer term, by resuming or maintaining agriculture at the levels permitted by drastically reduced trade and by an altered climate. Between several hundred million and about two thousand million people globally would be at risk of serious food shortages following a large nuclear exchange. The actual numbers of starving people, as well as the duration of the famines, depend on scenario assumptions. It is important to note, however, that famines, with possible mass death due to starvation, are likely to occur in non-combatant countries as well as in combatant ones, and even in countries remote from the theatres of war. The most vulnerable countries are developing nations in Africa, Asia and South America.

These conclusions of the SCOPE study are in general agreement with the findings of other independent studies, as well as with those of the 1980 United Nations study. They all note that eventually the victims of the indirect, large-scale and long-term effects of a major nuclear war would far outnumber the victims of the immediate effects of the nuclear explosions.

F.
Possible protective measures

A number of nations, especially in Europe, have organized a civil defence to meet the demands of a conventional war, with or without additional features specifically designed for nuclear war situations. Basically, all measures aim at short-term needs.

Some of these measures could help to limit the number of immediate fatalities caused by a nuclear attack. In view of the large devastation that would be caused, however, especially if nuclear weapons were used directly against the population, available resources for post-attack relief could prove totally inadequate. The value of protective measures in the case of a major nuclear exchange is a matter of dispute. There are those, however, who contend that a war might turn out to be limited in some sense and that it would be reasonable to undertake such protective measures as are technically and economically feasible.

Civil defence could, for instance, be very effective in saving lives that would otherwise be lost to fall-out in a limited attack against hard targets. On the other hand, it would be far less effective in a war involving strikes against industry in cities, or against the civilian population as such. This holds true for non-nuclear-weapon States as well as nuclear-weapon States in a nuclear war. Even in countries that do not themselves come under a nuclear attack, civil defence would be needed to deal with fall-out from large numbers of nuclear explosions in neighbouring countries.

After a nuclear attack (and to some extent after fall-out contamination originating from an attack elsewhere) there would be a need for food, energy, medical supplies, clothing and provisional housing. Crisis stockpiling of basic supplies would be an important precaution for dealing with these difficulties during the first days or weeks. However, allocation and distribution of emergency supplies would have to be carefully planned.

In discussing the question of civil defence, some analysts have endeavoured to compare the Chernobyl nuclear reactor accident of 1986 with the possible aftermath of a nuclear war. Although the circumstances would be different because Chernobyl involved only a release of radiation, with no associated blast damage, they believe this experience points to the kind of difficulties that would ensue after a nuclear exchange. For example, at Chernobyl the civil defence efforts were inadequate to deal with the situation. In a nuclear war, the magnitude of the problems related to civil defence would be greatly increased.

Notes

1. For more detailed descriptions of a nuclear explosion of the type that was exploded in Hiroshima and Nagasaki, see the Committee for the Compilation of Materials on Damage Caused by the Atomic Bombs in Hiroshima and Nagasaki, *The Impact of the A-Bomb*, Tokyo, Iwanamu Shoten Publishers, 1985, pp. 59–84. For a theoretical scenario involving modern nuclear weapons, see Office of Technology Assessment (OTA), *The Effects of Nuclear War*, Washington, D.C., US Government Printing Office, 1979, pp. 13–48. For a technical discussion, see L. W. McNaught, *Nuclear Weapons and Their Effects*, London, Brasseys, 1984, chap. 3; as well as Samuel Glasstone and Philip J. Dolan, eds., *The Effects of Nuclear Weapons*, Washington, D.C., US Government Printing Office, 1977, chaps. I-IV.

2. For a weapon with a yield of 10 to 20 kt, i.e. that of the Hiroshima and Nagasaki bombs, the maximum radius is approximately 200 m and its development takes about one second.

3. See McNaught, *op. cit.*, pp. 26 and 27.

4. *Ibid.*, pp. 37–46. See also Glasstone and Dolan, *op. cit.*, pp. 282–296 and chap. VII in general.

5. See McNaught, *op. cit.*, pp. 79 and 80. See also Glasstone and Dolan, *op. cit.*, pp. 45-48, and chaps. III-V for extensive discussions of air blasts and their effects.

6. Ground-zero is the point on the Earth's surface where a nuclear weapon is detonated; for an airburst it is the point on the Earth's surface directly below the point of detonation.

7.   See McNaught, *op. cit.*, pp. 49-58. See also Glasstone and Dolan, *op. cit.*, chaps. VIII and IX.

8.   See McNaught, *op. cit.*, pp. 95-106. See also Glasstone and Dolan, *op. cit.*, chap. XI.

9.   See Glasstone and Dolan, *op. cit.*, pp. 594–608.

10. *Ibid.*, pp. 36–38.

11. *Ibid.*, pp. 33–38.

12. The uncertainties are illustrated by the bombings of Japan. The Hiroshima bomb, estimated to be 13 kt, killed and injured about twice as many people as a larger bomb, 22 kt, used in Nagasaki. The discrepancy between the two outcomes has been attributed to the different topography of the two cities.

13. See Glasstone and Dolan, *op. cit.*, pp. 96–105.

14. *Ibid.*, pp. 604–613.

15. See *Ibid.*, chap. XI, for an in-depth discussion of the electromagnetic pulse and its effects. See also McNaught, *op. cit.*, pp. 95–106, for a short technical discussion.

16. See *The Impact of the A-Bomb*, pp. 22 and 25, for Hiroshima and pp. 47 and 48 for Nagasaki casualty figures.

17. OTA, *The Effects of Nuclear War*, p. 37.

18. *Ibid.*

19. Numerical estimates were made for the United Nations Study Group at the Swedish National Defense Research Institute.

20. World Health Organization, *Effects of Nuclear War on Health and Health Services*, 2nd edition, Geneva, WHO, 1987, p. 22.

21. W. H. Daugherty, B. G. Levi and F. N. von Hippel, *Casualties Due to the Blast, Heat and Radioactive Fallout from Various Hypothetical Attacks on the US*, Princeton University, Center for Energy and Environmental Studies Report No. 198, 1986.

22. See *Comprehensive Study on Nuclear Weapons* (United Nations publication, Sales No. E.81.I.11), paras. 198–212. See also C. F. von Weizsäcker, ed., *Kriegsfolgen und Kriegsverhütung*, Munich, 1971; *Ambio* (Journal of the Swedish Royal Academy of Sciences), vol. XI, 2-3 (Special Issue) 1982, pp. 163–173; WHO, *Effects of Nuclear War on Health and Health Services*.

23. See Charles-Philippe David, *Debating Counterforce*, Boulder, Westview Press, 1987, especially pp. 165–214.

24. OTA, *The Effects of Nuclear War*. This study does not specify the numbers, yields and heights of burst of the nuclear weapons employed. Rather it is assumed that the attacks are sufficient to destroy all or a certain part of the other side's nuclear weapons installations.

25. *Ibid.*, pp. 31 and 32.

26. See Bennett Ramberg, *Nuclear Power Plants as Weapons for the Enemy*, Los Angeles, University of California Press, 1980. See also WHO, *Effects of Nuclear War on Health and Health Services*, pp. 50 and 51.

27. S. A. Fetter and K. Tsipis, *Scientific American*, 244, 33 (1981); J. Peterson, *The Aftermath*, Pantheon, New York, 1983; J. Rotblat, *Nuclear Radiation in Warfare*, SIPRI, Taylor and Francis, London, 1981.

28. See Ramberg, *op. cit.*, pp. 71–109.

29. See David R. Marples, *Chernobyl and Nuclear Power in the USSR*, New York, St. Martin's Press, 1986, pp. 115–152, for a discussion of the accident at Chernobyl.

30. WHO, *Effects of Nuclear War on Health and Health Services*.

31. For a discussion of the medical effects of nuclear war, see the WHO study; the National Academy of Sciences and Institute of Medicine, Frederic Solomon and Robert Q. Marston, eds., *The Medical Implications of Nuclear War*, Washington, D.C., National Academy of Sciences Press, 1985; Ruth Adams and Susan Cullen, eds., *The Final Epidemic, Physicians and Scientists on Nuclear War*, Chicago, Educational Foundation for Nuclear Science, Inc., 1981; also Saul Aronow, Frank R. Erwin and Victor W. Sidel, eds., *The Fallen Sky — Medical Consequences of Thermonuclear War*, New York, Hill and Wang, 1963; Glasstone and Dolan, *op. cit.*, for biological effects of nuclear weapons, chap. XII.

32. See Glasstone and Dolan, *op. cit.*, pp. 560–574. See also Jennifer Leaning, "Burn and blast casualties: triage in a nuclear War", in Solomon and Marston, eds., *op. cit.*, pp. 251–283.

33. *Ibid.*

34. For a discussion on radiation, see WHO, *Effects of Nuclear War on Health and Health Services*, pp. 18–20; Glasstone and Dolan, *op. cit.*, pp. 541–618; *The Impact of the A-Bomb*, chaps. 5, 6, and 8; Patricia Lindop and Joseph Rotblat, "Consequences of radioactive fallout" in Adams and Cullen, *op. cit.*, pp. 117–150; Joseph Rotblat, "Acute radiation mortality in a nuclear war", and David Greer and Lawrence Rifkin, "The immunological impact of nuclear warfare", both in Solomon and Marston, *op. cit.*, pp. 233–250 and pp. 317–328.

35. The LD 50/60, i.e. the dose that causes 50 per cent fatalities within 60 days, has been repeatedly revised downwards. In a situation where medical treatment is not available, it is now thought by radiologists to be about 2.3 Gy to the bone marrow. Under similar conditions, doses above 4.5 Gy should be considered lethal, with death generally occurring within a few weeks. Gy stands for gray, which is the internationally accepted unit for radiation dose. With regard to radiation from a nuclear explosion or from early fall-out, gray is approximately equivalent to sievert.

36. Man-sievert is a common unit for "collective equivalent dose", i.e. the average equivalent dose to a group of people, multiplied by the number of people in the group.

37. In this regard, it is of particular importance, especially for children, to prevent radioactive iodine-131 from entering the body within the first weeks or so, since it concentrates in the thyroid glands, with subsequent high risks of contracting thyroid cancer. If strontium-90 and caesium-137 are in ingested food, strontium will be deposited in the bone, causing possible bone cancer, leukaemia, etc., and caesium will be distributed roughly evenly throughout the body. See Glasstone and Dolan, *op. cit.*, pp. 583–587.

38. *Sources, Effects and Risks of Ionizing Radiation*, United Nations Scientific Committee on the Effects of Atomic Radiation 1988 report (United Nations publication, Sales No. E.88.IX.7).

39. See Leaning, *op. cit.*, and John Constable, "Burn casualties", in Adams and Cullen, *op. cit.*, pp. 182–191.

40. For example, in Hiroshima, more than 90 per cent of physicians and nurses in the city were killed by the explosion.

41. See Alexander Leaf, "Food and nutrition in the aftermath of nuclear war", in Solomon and Marston, *op. cit.*, pp. 284–289.

42. See Paul R. Ehrlich, Carl Sagan, *et al.*, eds., *The Cold and the Dark — The World After Nuclear War*, New York, Norton, 1984, in particular Carl Sagan's chapter on "The atmospheric and climatic consequences of nuclear war", pp. 1–40. See also the National Research Council, *The Effects on the Atmosphere of a Major Nuclear Exchange*, Washington, D.C., National Academy Press, 1985.

43. *Study on the Climatic and Other Global Effects of Nuclear War* (United Nations publication, Sales No. E.89.IX.1), paras. 22–24.

44. Then Director of the United States Arms Control and Disarmament Agency, Fred Iklé, is quoted in the *Bulletin of Atomic Scientists*, May 1975, p. 32, as saying:

    "We do know that nuclear explosions in the Earth's atmosphere would generate vast quantities of nitrogen oxides that surround the Earth. But we do not know how much ozone depletion would occur from a large number of nuclear explosions — it might be imperceptible, but it might be almost total. We do not know how long such depletion would last — less than one year, or over ten years. And above all, we do not know what this depletion would do to plants, animals and people. Perhaps it would merely increase the hazard of sunburn. Or perhaps it would destroy critical links of the intricate food chain of plants and animals, and thus the ecological structure that permits man to remain alive on this planet. All we know is that we do not know."

45. Mark A. Harwell and Thomas C. Hutchinson, *SCOPE 28: Environmental Consequences of Nuclear War, Vol. II, Ecological and Agricultural Effects*, Chichester, John Wiley, 1985.

VII
Nuclear weapons and international security

A.
Nuclear weapons and security concepts

The Charter of the United Nations, which took effect in the aftermath of the Second World War, has laid down a broad foundation for world peace and order in the post-war era and has envisaged mechanisms for its preservation. It declared as one of the Organization's purposes to maintain international peace and security and to that end to take effective collective measures for the prevention and removal of threats to peace. It also recognized the inherent right of States to individual or collective self-defence in case of an armed attack and noted that nothing in the Charter precluded the existence of regional arrangements for the maintenance of international peace and security as appropriate for regional action. This has enabled States in meeting their security concerns to place emphasis on those options envisaged in the Charter which best suited their perceived national requirements.

The emergence of nuclear weapons has, however, added another dimension in the consideration of the question of individual, regional and global security of States, resulting in a long-lasting debate on the subject matter. This debate reflects differences in attitude on the role of nuclear weapons in general, and their relevance for national and international security in particular.

An overwhelming majority of non-nuclear-weapon States have formally renounced the possibility of acquiring or possessing nuclear weapons by adhering to the 1968 Treaty on the Non-Proliferation of Nuclear Weapons or to the two existing treaties establishing regional nuclear-weapon-free zones, or to both of the above.

While not possessing nuclear weapons themselves, some of the non-nuclear-weapon States, through various arrangements, including regional military alliances, have associated themselves with respective nuclear-weapon States, thereby accepting the so-called "nuclear umbrella" as an element of their defence, and consider that in their circumstances nuclear deterrence is a means to prevent war, including nuclear war. Other non-nuclear-weapon States have excluded this option from their national security considerations and have taken the position that nuclear weapons would threaten the very survival of the human race if these weapons were ever used in a major conflict. Thus, different approaches to security have been pursued by different individual countries or groups of countries.

The United States and the Soviet Union have, in the process of seeking to strengthen their national security, built large stocks of nuclear weapons. Although China, France and the United Kingdom have relatively small numbers of these weapons, they also see nuclear weapons as making a fundamental contribution to their national security.

Other non-nuclear-weapon States question whether nuclear weapons contribute in a positive way to security and contend that their own security is threatened by the possibility of nuclear war, which, in their opinion, cannot be excluded as long as these weapons exist. In view of this these States hold that international peace and security cannot be fully guaranteed until the ultimate elimination of all nuclear weapons is attained. On their initiative, the General Assembly held its first special session devoted to disarmament in 1978, and adopted a Final Document that called upon all States, in particular the nuclear-weapon States, *inter alia*, to consider as soon as possible various proposals designed to secure the cessation of the nuclear arms race, the avoidance of the use of nuclear weapons and the prevention of nuclear war and thereby ensure that the survival of mankind is not endangered.[1]

Many proponents of the latter approach have renounced possession of nuclear weapons and pursue a policy of non-alignment or neutrality. In that context, they advocate alternative methods for strengthening international peace and security.

One of these methods is reflected in the concept of nuclear-weapon-free zones. The general objective of such arrangements would be to prevent the emergence of new nuclear-weapon States in the region concerned and to assure against nuclear attack on the countries comprising the zone, as well as to ensure generally the absence of nuclear weapons from the region, including their stationing. Many States believe that such zones offer the prospect of precluding nuclear weapons altogether from the considerations of the security of a region. It would be important to assure that there is no possibility of clandestine production or acquisition of nuclear weapons in such zones. Examples of successful regional agreements are the zones established in Latin America by the 1967 Treaty of Tlatelolco and in the South Pacific by the 1987 Treaty of Rarotonga (see chap. VIII).

A number of countries have advocated even broader approaches to regional security than nuclear-weapon-free zones. These are the concepts of "demilitarized zones" and "zones of peace". The 1959 Antarctic Treaty is the foremost example in the first case (see chap. VIII); in the second, discussions are taking place on the creation of zones of peace in the Indian Ocean, the Mediterranean and the South Atlantic.

In the 1980s, yet another approach to international security in the nuclear era emerged — the concept of common security.[2] According to the concept, the key to security lies in the willingness of nations to organize their security policies in co-operation with each other. The proponents of this concept felt that this process of co-operation should begin with the improvement of relations between the two major Powers, the United States and the Soviet Union, and the respective military alliances they belong to. They further suggested that the *rapprochement* and normalization of relations between them should be combined with negotiations for conventional and nuclear arms limitation agreements, which are now taking place. In this process, in their opinion, close attention should also be paid to the problem of underdevelopment, which might have wider repercussions by causing wars and thereby destabilizing international peace and security. This sentiment was amplified further by the States that participated in the 1987 International Conference on the Relationship between Disarmament and Development. The Final Document of that Conference noted that non-military threats to national security of States had moved to the forefront of global concern for international security.[3]

When discussing the question of international peace and security in the nuclear age, it is important to recall that the quantitative and qualitative growth of nuclear weapons has been chiefly a consequence of the long-standing tensions and distrust between East and West. The end of the decade of the 1980s has, however, seen a positive change in this relationship. The world is no longer bipolar but is rather moving in the direction of new multipolar political and economic relationships that could have a profound effect on international security. This trend is further reinforced by recent important progress and concrete results in the bilateral negotiations on nuclear weapons between the United States and the Soviet Union and in the negotiation on conventional weapons between NATO and the Warsaw Treaty Organization. Thus, there is a growing recognition that negotiated reductions to progressively lower levels of nuclear weapons are desirable and possible and that they have the most positive impact on international peace and the security of all.

B.
International security and quantitative and qualitative development of nuclear weapons

The discussions of international security in the nuclear era have, generally speaking, focused on four specific aspects of the issue: (a) quantitative and qualitative developments of nuclear weapons by the nuclear-weapon States; (b) possible acquisition of nuclear weapons by additional States; (c) geographical spread of the deployment of nuclear weapons; and (d) the prevention of accidental use of nuclear weapons.

As far as the nuclear-weapon States are concerned, a central issue in these debates has been the question of quantitative and qualitative developments of their stockpiles. The two major Powers have long acquired the potential of inflicting unacceptable levels of destruction on each other. Their main concern since has been whether one side might acquire the potential to deny the other side the capability for a disarming first-strike. This concern has been responsible in large measure for the fuelling of the nuclear arms competition.

As an illustration of this phenomenon, it is pointed out that, according to academic sources, in 1967 the United States possessed some 4,500 strategic warheads while the Soviet Union had approximately 1,000.[4] However, it is estimated that by 1990 these stockpiles may have increased up to 13,000 for the United States and 11,500 for the Soviet Union.[5] This growth involved both quantitative and qualitative aspects (see chap. II).

The number of nuclear delivery vehicles and deployed warheads is expected to drop significantly as a result of the destruction of one whole category of nuclear weapons under the terms of the 1987 Treaty on the Elimination of Intermediate-Range and Shorter-Range Missiles (INF Treaty) and the anticipated reductions within the framework of the strategic arms reduction talks (START) expected to be concluded by the end of 1990. At the same time, both major Powers are continuing to make technological improvements in the quality of their nuclear weapons.

For example, it is widely believed that the United States Trident-II missile, when deployed, would have about the same accuracy as the majority of currently deployed ICBMs.[6] It is also expected that the Soviet SLBMs will attain comparable accuracy as well (see chap. III). Some analysts believe that both sides will have the capability of achieving a high probability of destruction of any hardened land targets. These developments are related to the perception that, owing to the survivability of SSBNs, their increased accuracy would only enhance nuclear deterrence.

There are those, however, who point out that the shorter flight times and accuracy of the SLBMs may increase fears of a surprise attack. They also note that the increased deployment of strategic cruise missiles, both ALCMs and SLCMs, may represent a further complicating factor because of their accuracy and the unpredictability of their flight patterns.[7]

In addition to developments in technology directly related to weapons (see chap. III), advances in other areas also have important implications for national strategic policies of those States which have those weapons. Improvements, for example, in the capability of the command, control and communication systems for the strategic nuclear forces include quicker and more accurate observation by satellites and radars, enabling enhanced warning of attack.

Making an overall assessment of the full implications of all the qualitative improvements is difficult since the various developments appear capable of both contributing to and weakening stability. Thus, for instance, in spite of the technological advances in the weapons industry, a pre-emptive strike against submarine-based missiles at sea or a strategic airforce that maintains a substantive airborne alert would not be effective.

As progress is made in the negotiations between the two major Powers regarding their nuclear strategic forces, more questions are likely to be asked with regard to the future of the nuclear weapons of the other nuclear-weapon States. These three States — China, France and the United Kingdom — although possessing significant nuclear weaponry, still have less than 10 per cent of the total nuclear weapons in the world.[8]

In the 1980s, China, France and the United Kingdom began to modernize and expand their nuclear forces. The United Kingdom plans to buy Trident missiles, which would greatly enhance the accuracy and destructive power of any single British SSBN.[9] France has launched its own maritime and land-based nuclear weapon modernization programmes. It is estimated that both Powers will have the potential to deploy some 500 warheads on their SSBNs.[10] China has also increased its nuclear forces, but not as much as France and the United Kingdom.

The position of the United Kingdom and France is that they could participate in negotiations on their nuclear weapons only if the overall threat to their national security was significantly reduced and, in particular, if the disparity between the nuclear arsenals of the two principal nuclear Powers and their respective arsenals was substantially reduced. They believe, furthermore, that negotiations on nuclear weapons could not be conducted without taking into consideration the threat of chemical weapons and conventional armaments.

China holds the view that the two major nuclear Powers should take the lead in halting the testing, qualitative development, production and deployment of all types of nuclear weapons and in drastically reducing and eliminating them. After that, a broadly representative international conference on nuclear disarmament, with the participation of all nuclear States, could be held to examine steps and measures for the complete elimination of all nuclear weapons.

C.
International security and possible emergence of new nuclear-weapon States

Apart from the five, no other State in the world has been officially declared to be a nuclear-weapon State. In 1974, India detonated a nuclear device. While this explosion demonstrated India's capability to develop nuclear weapons eventually, India declared that it was carried out for peaceful purposes.

As already noted, an overwhelming number of non-nuclear-weapon States have also undertaken a formal commitment not to acquire nuclear weapons. Consequently, the discussion of various aspects of international security as related to this group of countries is limited to two basic issues: how to maintain an effective régime for non-proliferation of nuclear weapons without adversely affecting other, peaceful applications of nuclear technology; and how to bring into this régime all those countries which have not yet formally renounced the option of acquiring nuclear weapons, particularly those which are considered to have technical capability to do so or which may have such ambitions.

Under the terms of the Treaty on the Non-Proliferation of Nuclear Weapons (NPT), non-nuclear-weapon States parties agree to apply safeguards administered by the International Atomic Energy Agency (IAEA) to all their peaceful nuclear activities in order to ensure that fissionable material is not diverted to nuclear explosive purposes. As at February 1990, safeguards agreements were in force for 83 of the 138 non-nuclear-weapon States party to the NPT. Of these, 41 States have no nuclear activity and no nuclear material or facility in operation. Fifty-four non-nuclear-weapon States party to the NPT have not as yet concluded the required safeguards agreement pursuant to article III.4 of the Treaty. In 1989 the Agency applied safeguards in 42 non-nuclear-weapon States party to the NPT and in one State pursuant to the Tlatelolco Treaty.[11]

The Treaties of Tlatelolco and Rarotonga, respectively, also provide for IAEA safeguards. Some 18 of the 23 Latin American States party to the Treaty of Tlatelolco have concluded safeguards agreements with IAEA, as have two States with territories in the zone of application of this Treaty. Safeguards agreements under the NPT have been concluded with 8 of the 11 signatories of the Rarotonga Treaty.[12]

IAEA also administers the original system of safeguards in accordance with its statute, whereby member States can accept safeguards on nuclear material in specific facilities or on particular quantities of nuclear material.

In recent years, there has been extensive debate about non-proliferation and the basis of nuclear trade in general. Because of the possible connection between peaceful and military nuclear technologies, nuclear facilities and international trade in nuclear materials are subject to a wide range of international controls to provide assurance that nuclear industries are not being used for development of nuclear weapons. States that are major nuclear suppliers have adopted the position that nuclear materials, technology and equipment that could be used for development of nuclear weapons should not be supplied without the recipient State agreeing to apply IAEA safeguards and accept other conditions.[13] Some have adopted stringent national policies designed to seek specific assurances that nuclear co-operation would not lead or contribute to development of a nuclear-weapon capability. Other nuclear suppliers also require IAEA safeguards and the commitment by the recipient countries to peaceful uses for their nuclear exports. A number of States now require acceptance of so-called "full-scope" safeguards or adherence to the non-proliferation Treaty or another binding international commitment not to acquire nuclear weapons as a condition for significant nuclear co-operation.

At the end of 1989, 172 safeguards agreements were in force with 102 States. In 59 States with significant nuclear activities, 924 installations and related facilities were under safeguards or contained safeguarded materials at year-end 1989, including the five nuclear-weapon States, where safeguards were actually implemented in 8 nuclear installations.[14]

International consensus exists that, although measures are necessary to prevent the proliferation of nuclear weapons, all States have the right to develop nuclear energy for peaceful purposes. Concern has, however, been expressed by some that the conditions governing access to nuclear technology, equipment, material and services do not sufficiently recognize the fact that national security and development may depend initially on secure access to energy resources. Many States have criticized some policies of supplier States. Their objective in the international discussion of these issues is the search for an agreed basis whereby their desire for fullest access to technology for development is reconciled with the need to insure against the further spread of nuclear weapons.

As regards specifically the question of the acquisition of nuclear weapons by additional States, concerns have been expressed on different occasions and in various contexts, that some non-nuclear-weapon States might develop nuclear-weapon programmes. This concern was expressed particularly in connection with the so-called "threshold" States. Since many countries, most notably industrially highly developed ones and possibly some others, have both technical capability and resources to become nuclear-weapon States, but have not demonstrated any intention in that respect, the term "threshold" usually applies only to those countries which have in various ways demonstrated such intentions or are believed to be pursuing such an objective.

Notwithstanding these concerns, there has been no formal request to put in motion mechanisms envisaged under any of the existing non-proliferation arrangements with a view to clarifying the activities of the countries in question covered by such arrangements. In this connection, it should be noted that neither at the Third Review Conference of the Parties to the Treaty on the Non-Proliferation of Nuclear Weapons, in 1985, nor during the preparatory stages for the Fourth Review Conference taking place in August/September 1990 has the question of the possible non-compliance of the parties been formally raised. This is also the case regarding the formal discussions in IAEA as well as within the framework of the two regional nuclear-weapon-free zones.

The situation is different regarding the second group of countries, that is, those which are not covered by such arrangements. Several of them are located in areas affected by local tensions and mutual suspicions that have given rise to concerns that some of these countries might, in fact, be interested in or even actively pursuing a nuclear-weapon option.

The nuclear programmes of India and Pakistan have been the subject of international concern. Neither country is covered by the existing non-proliferation arrangements, although the Governments of both India and Pakistan have repeatedly reaffirmed their interest in peaceful aspects of nuclear technology only.

Two specific situations have, however, been formally brought to the attention of the United Nations. One concerns Israel and the other South Africa. Neither of these countries is a party to the existing arrangements regarding the non-proliferation of nuclear weapons and both maintain unsafeguarded nuclear installations.

The report on Israeli nuclear armament submitted to the General Assembly in 1987 restated the conclusion of the 1981 Study on Israeli nuclear armament, which noted that, although there was no conclusive proof that Israel possessed nuclear weapons, there was no doubt "that Israel, if it has not already crossed that threshold, has the capability to manufacture nuclear weapons within a very short time".[15] Israel's official position in this respect is neither to confirm nor to deny its nuclear-weapon capability. Israel has, on various occasions, formally stated that it would not be the first to introduce nuclear weapons into the Middle East and that it does not co-operate on nuclear matters with South Africa.[16]

The report on South Africa's nuclear capability was submitted to the General Assembly in 1981.[17] Among other conclusions, the report noted that South Africa had the technical capability to manufacture nuclear weapons and that its reactors and enrichment plants had not been placed under IAEA safeguards. Yearly since then, the General Assembly has passed a resolution requesting the Secretary-General to keep it informed regarding new developments in this connection. [18] In August 1988, the Foreign Minister of South Africa declared that his country had the capability to make nuclear weapons.[19] Nevertheless, there is no proof that South Africa has built any weapons yet. South Africa has discussed the possibility of acceding to the Non-Proliferation Treaty with the depositaries on a number of occasions. At its 1990 session, the United Nations Disarmament Commission adopted by consensus a report on South Africa's nuclear capability.[20]

Since the beginning of the 1980s, another concern has been expressed in connection with the activities of the so-called "threshold" countries, namely, the possibility that they might also be developing ballistic missile technology. Such missiles provide the most dependable means of delivering nuclear weapons. The whole matter is further complicated by the fact that the missile technology has also many other military applications not related to nuclear-weapon capabilities as well as in the area of peaceful activities. Many States are acquiring this technology through foreign acquisitions or indigenous productions either for military or civilian purposes.

In recent times a number of States have taken steps on the national as well as on the multilateral level to curb the spread of ballistic missiles. In April 1987, Canada, France, the Federal Republic of Germany, Italy, Japan, the United Kingdom and the United States adopted a régime of parallel export controls designed to counter the proliferation of ballistic missiles or unmanned systems (such as cruise missiles) capable of delivering a 500 kg payload at least 300 km. This régime, entitled the Missile Technology Control Régime (MTCR), also controls export of various missile technologies such as guidance devices, individual rocket stages and re-entry vehicles. Importers of missile technology for approved programmes may be required to provide assurances to signatory nations that such technology will not be used for proscribed programmes.[21] In the last year, Belgium, Luxembourg, the Netherlands and Spain have joined and Australia announced its intention to join the MTCR.

In 1988, the Soviet Union and the United States started bilateral discussions on the problems of the proliferation of missile technology, and the United States has discussed the issue with other countries as part of its efforts to strengthen the international nuclear non-proliferation régime. The Soviet Union affirmed its support for the objectives of the MTCR in the Joint Statement issued on 4 June 1990 at the summit meeting between President Bush and President Gorbachev.

D.
International security and geographical spread of nuclear weapons

The nuclear-weapon States maintain their nuclear forces in various deployment areas. Two of them — the United States and the Soviet Union — on the basis of bilateral or other arrangements, deploy their forces, including nuclear, at military bases and installations also on the territories of other States. The nuclear-weapon States also use the high seas and international air space for their ships and aircraft that carry on board nuclear weapons. Some of these ships and aircraft call at ports of other States and make stops at their airports. Thus, at any given time there are a number of nuclear weapons present in the areas beyond the national territory of the nuclear-weapon States themselves. Some aspects of this geographical spread of nuclear weapons have been the subject of continuing discussions and differences in positions.

The majority of non-nuclear-weapon States do not permit the deployment of nuclear weapons on their territory. For many of these States, this policy also applies to nuclear weapons on board ships and aircraft on visits to their territory. Many of them also express concern about the use of international waterways and airspace on the grounds that the presence of nuclear weapons there in various ways, such as through accidents, may endanger international security.

In addition, many non-nuclear-weapon States do not allow warships carrying nuclear weapons to pass through their internal waters so as not to participate in or assist the spread of nuclear weapons. They also do so in order to preclude the possibility of increasing regional tensions and to avoid the various hazards that may arise, particularly the exposure of their peoples to nuclear contamination at a time when they do not possess the material or technical capabilities to counter such dangers. To allow passage in such circumstances would constitute an evasion of their responsibility towards their peoples.

The position of the nuclear-weapon States on the issues raised reflects their different policies regarding the deployment of nuclear weapons. Thus, generally speaking, the nuclear-weapon States emphasize their rights under international law to free navigation of the high seas for their naval vessels, including those which may be carrying nuclear weapons, in accordance with the United Nations Convention on the Law of the Sea.[22]

A majority of the nuclear-weapon States maintain a policy of neither confirming nor denying (NCND) the presence of nuclear weapons on board their ships and aircraft in any particular place at any particular time. Of the approximately 14,600 nuclear warheads reportedly earmarked for naval and maritime deployment, 9,200 are on ballistic missiles deployed on submarines that would rarely be carried to foreign ports. The remaining 5,400 tactical and strategic weapons are the focus of the NCND issue.[23]

The United States says that the purpose of the policy, *inter alia*, is to "withhold from a potential enemy information that could be used against US forces in the event of a conflict".[24]

The policies of France and the United Kingdom are similar to that of the United States. To date China has not deployed tactical nuclear weapons on surface vessels.

The Soviet Union offered in 1988, on the basis of reciprocity with the United States and other nuclear Powers, to announce the presence or absence of nuclear weapons on board its naval vessels calling at foreign ports.[25]

Currently, the only way to determine whether a ship is actually carrying nuclear weapons is through on-site inspection, although there is a debate about the feasibility of determining the absence of nuclear weapons from a ship by remote sensing.[26] As naval ships enjoy sovereign immunity and are exempt under international law from inspections and search by host Governments, States that accept NCND leave the determination of whether to dock to the discretion of the nuclear-weapon State.

In recent years there has been growing public opposition in many countries to visits of ships that may be carrying nuclear weapons. In addition, the policy of neither confirming nor denying makes it difficult to be certain whether or not naval vessels involved in accidents were armed with nuclear weapons.

Also, the difficulty to be certain whether or not naval vessels were armed with nuclear weapons owing to the NCND practice was referred to in resolution 170 (VIII) of the General Conference of the Latin-American Organization for the Proscription of Nuclear Weapons of 19 May 1983 within the context of information concerning the introduction of nuclear weapons during the course of the South Atlantic conflict in 1982.

Certain States have drawn up regulations concerning visits of nuclear-armed or nuclear-powered ships. In 1987, New Zealand adopted legislation stipulating that a visit would be granted only "if the Prime Minister is satisfied that the warships will not be carrying any nuclear explosive devices upon their entry into the internal waters of New Zealand".[27] Thus a nuclear-capable ship can be admitted to New Zealand ports as long as it is not actually carrying nuclear weapons. Although New Zealand does not openly challenge NCND, but rather makes its own assessment of whether nuclear weapons are carried on a particular vessel, France, the United Kingdom and the United States have chosen not to propose warship visits to New Zealand.

In New Zealand's view, prohibiting nuclear-weapon-carrying and nuclear-powered ships emanates from its wish not to be defended by nuclear weapons and its belief that nuclear weapons do not have a role in the South Pacific (see chap. VIII regarding the Treaty of Rarotonga). However, because New Zealand's ship visit policy is based on particular regional security considerations, the New Zealand Government has declared repeatedly that it is not intended as a model for other States to follow.[28]

E.
Prevention of accidental use of nuclear weapons

Since the early days of nuclear weapons, nuclear-weapon States have been interested in avoiding any unauthorized or accidental use of nuclear weapons. Many safeguards have been introduced by nuclear-weapon States either unilaterally or by agreement. The nuclear warheads themselves have been designed to preclude accidental detonation as a result of exposure to mechanical damage, heat, blast or radiation. Technical designs and procedural rules (see chap. III), have been developed to preserve effective control over nuclear weapons and related operations.

These efforts have been successful in the sense that no accidental or unauthorized nuclear-weapon explosion has occurred during the several decades in which up to 60,000 nuclear weapons have been handled. While nuclear weapons have been involved in a number of accidents, none of them has ever exploded.

Although the risks of intentional nuclear war between the two major military alliances are considered to be low and steadily decreasing, it is considered that accidents might initiate a nuclear war unintentionally. In its broadest sense, the term accidental nuclear war would include any way a nuclear war could start in response to false signals, incorrect or misinterpreted information, an unauthorized, accidental or terrorist launch or uncontrolled escalation of a conventional conflict. Technical malfunctioning, human error or irrational decisions under stress could contribute to the risk.

1.
Protective measures

As described in chapter II, the control of nuclear weapons has been highly centralized in all countries concerned. Complex procedures have been developed to secure continuous contact and authentic messages. Special control has been organized by nuclear-weapon States for weapons deployed outside their territory. One form of permissive action links (PAL) consists of a highly secure coded signal from the highest political level to be inserted in the weapons before they can be used.[29]

The hotline between Moscow and Washington was established in 1963 after the Cuban missile crisis in order to reduce the risk of nuclear war by accident, miscalculation or failure of communication. It has been improved several times. Similar hotlines have been established between Moscow and London, and Moscow and Paris. Several agreements between the United States and the Soviet Union have been concluded for the purpose of avoiding military confrontation and provocative behaviour and of giving advance notification before missiles are tested (see chap. VIII).

The positive effect of these measures, however, runs the risk of being counteracted by developments in nuclear weapons systems. As a consequence, further protective measures are needed. The most essential measures must be based on an evaluation of the command and control system.

2.
Possible triggers to an accidental war

Improvements in satellite-based photo-reconnaissance, ballistic missile guidance, the introduction of multiple warheads on missiles and the development of anti-satellite systems tend to make nuclear weapons and the command and control system vulnerable to attack. With only a very limited part of its strategic nuclear forces one of the major nuclear-weapon Powers could conceivably knock out the command and control system of its adversary (a "decapitating" strike).

In a situation of perceived severe crisis, these developments could give a high premium on striking first or striking back when indications of enemy attack are received (launch on warning). There would then be only a very short time for information-handling, decision-making and launching, since an intercontinental missile has a flight time of about 30 minutes and a submarine-based missile could approach half of that.[30]

The command and control system is designed to enable the early detection and intepretation of any hostile acts so that an appropriate response can be made (see chap. II). The increasing sophistication of nuclear weapons in terms of higher accuracy and reduced flight times has greatly increased the difficulty of producing an integrated system capable of ensuring firm political control and effective military use of such weapons. In the command and control system false signals occasionally occur that are sorted out by comparing indications from different sensors. In a crisis situation with a perceived immediate threat, false or misinterpreted signals, lost connections, unidentified use of weapons combined with short time for cross-checking and decision-making could lead to mistaken decisions and to accidental nuclear war.[31]

There have been numerous reports of false warnings due to various causes. They include misinterpretations caused by atmospheric disturbances, a meteorite shower, a flight of wild geese and a computer chip failure.[32] In the systems used in the Soviet Union and the United States, however, any warning has to be confirmed by a second independent sensor system using a different physical technique for observation.[33]

The reliability of military electronics is an increasingly important problem. There are at least three general types of electronic failures that have been well documented. The first involves items of electronic hardware. The second involves problems of interference with the electromagnetic environment in which the military systems operate. The third type of electronic failure is manifest in computer software. The larger and more complex a computer programme becomes, the more difficult it is to have confidence in the programme working correctly under all possible conditions.

Both machines and humans may be fallible, especially in wartime conditions. Chaos, stress, sleep deprivation, isolation and even drug or alcohol abuse may cause inaccurate judgements. Nevertheless, thus far there have been no reported losses, thefts or detonations of nuclear devices as a result of these problems.

Notes

1. See resolution S-10/2, para. 58. See also *The United Nations Disarmament Yearbook*, vol. 3, 1978 (United Nations publication, Sales No. E.79.XI.3).
2. *Common Security — A Blueprint For Survival*, report of the Independent Commission on Disarmament Security Issues (A/CN.10/38).
3. A/CONF.130/39.
4. *Comprehensive Study on Nuclear Weapons* (United Nations publication, Sales No. E.81.I.11), para. 403.
5. *SIPRI Yearbook 1990: World Armaments and Disarmament*, New York, Oxford University Press, 1990, pp. 14 and 16.
6. Bernard Blake, ed., *Jane's Weapons Systems 1988–89*, Surrey, Jane's Information Group Ltd., 1984, pp. 30 and 906.
7. See Charles A. Sorrels, *US Cruise Missile Programs: Development, Deployment and Implications for Arms Control*, Oxford, Brassey's Defence Publishers, Ltd., 1983, pp. 3, 4, 8 and 9. See also Richard K. Betts, ed., *Cruise Missiles: Technology, Strategy and Politics*, Washington, D.C., Brookings Institution, 1981.
8. For British, French and Chinese totals, see *SIPRI Yearbook, 1990*, pp. 20–23.
9. See *SIPRI Yearbook 1988*, p. 47.
10. For information on the British SSBN programme, see *Ibid*. For information on the French programme, see *SIPRI Yearbook 1989*, p. 31 and *SIPRI Yearbook 1988*, p. 51.
11. See NPT/CONF.IV/12. Nuclear-weapon States parties to the Treaty are not required to place their nuclear facilities under safeguards. Some civilian nuclear facilities in the five nuclear-weapon States are safeguarded under so-called "voluntary offer" agreements concluded with IAEA. The entry into force of these agreements are: United Kingdom, August 1978; United States, December

1980; France, September 1981; USSR, June 1985; and China, September 1989. IAEA safeguards are applied in nuclear-weapon States in a limited number of facilities selected by IAEA. See also Leonard Spector, *The Undeclared Bomb*, Cambridge, Mass., Ballinger Publishers, 1988, p. 73.

12. *IAEA News Features*, special edition, Vienna, Austria, April 1990.

13. The Nuclear Suppliers Group — Belgium, Canada, Czechoslovakia, France, Germany, Federal Republic of, German Democratic Republic, Italy, Japan, Netherlands, Poland, Sweden, Switzerland, USSR, United Kingdom and United States — notified IAEA in 1978 of common guidelines to be applied in the export of nuclear material equipment or technology. See also Spector, *op. cit.*, pp. 9, 10, 315 and 316.

14. *IAEA News Features*, special edition, Vienna, Austria, April 1990.

15. See the report of the Secretary-General on Israeli nuclear armament (A/42/581), p. 2.

16. *United Nations Disarmament Yearbook*, vol. 12, 1987 (United Nations publication, Sales No. E.88.IX.2), chap. X.

17. *South Africa's Plan and Capability in the Nuclear Field* (United Nations publication, Sales No. E.81.I.10).

18. The resolutions were adopted with the following voting results: 40/89 A (148-0-6); 41/55 A (150-0-5); 42/34 A (151-0-4); 43/71 A (151-0-4); 44/113 A (147-0-4); 40/89 B (135-4-14); 41/55 B (139-4-13); 42/34 B (140-4-13); 43/71 B (138-4-12); and 44/113 B (137-4-10).

19. *The New York Times*, 14 August 1988, "Pretoria says it can build A-arms". p. A16. Botha was quoted at a Vienna press conference as saying "we have the capability to make one. We have the capability to do so, should we want to".

20. *Official Records of the General Assembly, Forty-fifth Session, Supplement No. 42* (A/45/42).

21. See Jozef Goldblat, *Twenty Years of the Non-Proliferation Treaty, Implementation and Prospects*, International Peace Research Institute, Oslo, 1990.

22. See *The Law of the Sea* (United Nations publication, Sales No. E.83.V.5). Regarding territorial seas, see part II; regarding international navigation, see part III.

23. *Bulletin of the Atomic Scientists*, vol. 55, No. 7, September 1989, p. 48.

24. R. Fieldhouse, ed., *Security at Sea: Naval Forces and Arms Control*, Oxford, Oxford University Press, 1990, p. 247.

25. *Official Records of the General Assembly, Fifteenth Special Session, Supplement No. 2* (A/S-15/PV.12).

26. At the same time, work is now in progress to find methods to detect with assurance the presence of nuclear weapons on board ships by means of distant verification equipment. In 1989, a joint experiment in the Black Sea was conducted by the USSR Academy of Sciences and the American private organization, the United States Natural Resource Defense Council, in co-operation with the Soviet navy. See Thomas B. Cochran, "Black Sea experiment only a start" in *Bulletin of the Atomic Scientists*, vol. 45, No. 9, November 1989, pp. 12–16. See also the technical report by Steven Fetter, Thomas B. Cochran, Lee Grodzins, Harvey Lynch and Martin Zucker, "Gamma-Ray measurements of a Soviet cruise-missile warhead" (April 1990 pre-publication draft from NRDC, forthcoming in *Science*).

27. New Zealand Nuclear-Free-Zone, Disarmament, and Arms Control Act 1987 (No. 86), clause 9. In 1985 New Zealand had refused entry to the US destroyer

USS Buchanan because its non-nuclear status was not guaranteed. This refusal resulted in the break-up of the ANZUS alliance (the security Treaty between Australia, New Zealand and the United States) in August 1987. Under the legislation a general prohibition also applies to nuclear-powered vessels.

28. Prime Minister David Lange said in 1987 "You cannot simply export a model based on our own particular security considerations". Ministry of Foreign Affairs Press Statement No. 8, 19 June 1987, p. 12.

29. See Donald R. Cotter, "Peacetime operations: safety and security", in Ashton B. Carter, John D. Steinbruner and Charles A. Zraket, eds., *Managing Nuclear Operations*, Washington, D.C., Broookings Institution, 1987, pp. 46-51. See also Albert Wohlstetter and Richard Brody, "Continuing control as a requirement for deterring", p. 168 in the same volume.

30. See Thomas B. Cochran, William A. Arkin and Milton M. Hoenig, *Nuclear Weapons Databook: Vol. 1, United States Nuclear Forces and Capabilities*, Cambridge, Mass., Ballinger Publishers, 1984, p. 100. See also Theodore A. Postol, "Targeting", in Carter, *et al., op. cit.*, p. 388, and Barry R. Schneider, Colin S. Gray and Keith B. Payne, eds., *Missiles for the Nineties: ICBMs and Strategic Policy*, Boulder, Westview Press, 1984, pp. 9 and 10.

31. See Bruce G. Blair, "Alerting in crisis and conventional war", in Carter *et al., op. cit.*, pp. 75-120.

32. See John May, *The Greenpeace Book of the Nuclear Age: The Hidden History, The Human Cost*, New York, Pantheon/Greenpeace Communications Ltd., 1989.

33. See Ashton B. Carter, "Sources of error and uncertainty", in Carter *et al., op. cit.*, pp. 611-639.

VIII
Nuclear arms limitation and disarmament

A.
Introduction

Since the dawn of the nuclear age almost half a century ago, efforts have been made in the world community to deal with the various implications of the existence of nuclear weapons. Many of them have been concerned with a wide range of specific measures aimed at the limitation, reduction and elimination of nuclear weapons and their delivery systems. Some others dealt with the prevention of the proliferation of nuclear weapons, cessation of nuclear-weapon tests, and the establishment of nuclear-weapon-free zones in various regions of the world. Some discussions focused also on the legal rules regarding possession and possible use of nuclear weapons.

Arms limitation and disarmament efforts have been pursued both within and outside the United Nations framework. The United States and the Soviet Union have considered a number of measures bilaterally, particularly those dealing with the limitations of their strategic arms and the elimination of their intermediate/medium-range nuclear missiles (INF). Many other efforts were undertaken in the regional as well as global context. Over the years, a number of agreements have been reached dealing with various aspects of nuclear weapons.

B.
Constraints on the possession of nuclear weapons

Two different approaches developed with respect to imposing constraints on the acquisition of nuclear weapons. Both of them deal with the acquisition of nuclear weapons by non-nuclear-weapon States. One approach involved negotiations for a global treaty committing nuclear-weapon States not to transfer nuclear weapons and non-nuclear-weapon States not to acquire them. The other approach concerned the establishment of nuclear-weapon-free zones in various regions of the world. Although based on the same principle of non-acquisition of nuclear weapons, the latter approach encompasses additional constraints, both on nuclear and non-nuclear States parties to such zones and is, as such, broader in scope.

120

1.

Treaty on the Non-Proliferation of Nuclear Weapons

The Non-Proliferation Treaty (resolution 2373 (XXII), annex) is regarded by many as an important achievement in the area of nuclear-arms regulation. The Treaty was opened for signature on 1 July 1968 and entered into force on 5 March 1970. Among the nuclear-weapon States, the Soviet Union, the United Kingdom and the United States are parties to the Treaty and serve as its depositaries. China and France, while not parties to the Treaty, have on various occasions stated that they do not support nuclear proliferation and would not act contrary to the Treaty's provisions. By the end of June 1990 the Treaty had 141 parties, making it the most widely accepted arms limitation instrument. A considerable number of non-nuclear-weapon States advanced in nuclear technology have become parties to the Treaty. On the other hand, some such States have not yet become party to it.

The basic provisions of the Treaty are to: prevent the spread of nuclear weapons (arts. I and II); provide assurance, through international safeguards, that the peaceful nuclear activities of non-nuclear-weapon States will not be diverted to making such weapons (art. III); facilitate, to the maximum extent consistent with the other purposes of the Treaty, the peaceful uses of nuclear energy through full co-operation — with the potential benefits of any peaceful application of nuclear explosion technology being made available to non-nuclear parties under appropriate international observation (arts. IV and V); express the determination to pursue negotiations in good faith on effective measures relating to cessation of the nuclear-arms race at an early date and to nuclear disarmament, and on a treaty on general and complete disarmament under strict and effective international control (art. VI). The NPT also has considerable relevance to several other arms control and disarmament measures, e.g. a comprehensive nuclear-test ban, negative security assurances and nuclear-weapon-free zones.

The Treaty also contains provisions for periodic review of its operation (art. VIII). It also states that a conference shall be convened 25 years following the entry into force (i.e. in 1995) "to decide whether the Treaty shall continue in force indefinitely, or shall be extended for an additional fixed period or periods" (art. X).

Three review conferences have been held so far: in 1975, 1980 and 1985. The Fourth Review Conference is scheduled to take place in August/September 1990. China and France have indicated their intention to attend as observers.

At the time of the Third Review Conference there were 131 parties to the Treaty. The strong convergence of interests of the nuclear and non-nuclear-weapon States parties to check the further spread of nuclear weapons provided a basis for the successful conclusion of the Conference with the adoption by consensus of a Final Document. This document, although critical of the implementation of the Treaty in some areas and recommending further strengthening of the international system for non-proliferation in others, confirmed unanimously the sustained validity of the fundamental aims of the Treaty and concluded that it continues to meet its basic objective.[1]

2.
Nuclear-weapon-free zones

The idea of establishing nuclear-weapon-free zones as a means of keeping the regions concerned free of nuclear weapons began to attract the attention of the international community in the 1950s. Many proposals have been made since that time. While some of them are still being considered in various forums, agreement has been reached on two of them.

a.
Treaty of Rarotonga[2]

The South Pacific Nuclear Free Zone Treaty (Treaty of Rarotonga) was opened for signature on 6 August 1985 and entered into force on 11 December 1986. Eleven out of 15 members of the South Pacific Forum had become parties to the Treaty as at June 1990. The four countries that have not signed the Treaty are: Tonga, Vanuatu, the Federated States of Micronesia and the Republic of the Marshall Islands. The Treaty area encompasses large sea areas, but most provisions apply only on land and, consequently, nothing in the Treaty affects the exercise of the rights of any State under international law with regard to freedom of the seas.

The Treaty of Rarotonga creates a "nuclear-free", rather than a "nuclear-weapon-free", zone. The prime intention of the Treaty was to keep the region free of the stationing of nuclear weapons, nuclear testing and environmental pollution by radioactive waste. Moreover, the parties wished to prohibit all types of nuclear explosions. Accordingly, the operative articles of the Treaty refer consistently to "nuclear explosive devices", a term which covers all nuclear devices, irrespective of the purpose, military or peaceful, which has been given for their existence.

Each party to the Treaty undertakes not to manufacture, acquire, possess or have control over any nuclear explosive device inside or outside the zone. Moreover, it undertakes to conduct any nuclear co-operation with other States in accordance with strict non-proliferation measures to provide assurance of exclusively peaceful non-explosive use, and to support the effectiveness of the international non-proliferation system based on the Non-Proliferation Treaty and the safeguards system of IAEA. While exercising its sovereign rights to decide for itself whether to allow foreign ships (which may be nuclear-powered or nuclear-armed) to visit its ports or foreign aircraft to visit its airfields or fly over its territory, each party undertakes to prevent any nuclear explosive device from being stationed in its territory. It also undertakes to prevent all testing of such devices on its territory and not to assist others in doing so. It further undertakes not to dump radioactive wastes anywhere at sea within the zone and to prevent such dumping or storing by anyone in its territorial sea.

The States outside the zone that have jurisdiction over territories within it (France, the United Kingdom and the United States) would, upon becoming parties to Protocol 1, apply the Treaty's key provisions to those territories. The five nuclear-weapon States would, upon becoming parties to Protocol 2, undertake not to use or threaten to use nuclear explosive devices against parties to the Treaty, and any such State would, upon becoming party to Protocol 3, refrain from nuclear testing within the zone.

The Soviet Union and China have ratified Protocols 2 and 3. France, the United Kingdom and the United States have indicated that they do not intend at this time to become parties to any of the Protocols. However, the United States declared that none of its practices and activities within the Treaty area were inconsistent with the Treaty and its Protocols, while the United Kingdom stated that it would respect the intentions of States of the region on Protocols 1 and 3.[3]

South Pacific nations have expressed disappointment that France has not signed the Protocol 3 and continues to test within the zone. France put forward its position on this matter to the General Assembly on 2 June 1988.[4]

b.

Treaty of Tlatelolco[5]

The Treaty for the Prohibition of Nuclear Weapons in Latin America (Treaty of Tlatelolco) was the first treaty to establish a nuclear-weapon-free zone in a densely populated area. It was also the first agreement to establish a system of international control and a permanent supervisory organ, the Agency for the Prohibition of Nuclear Weapons in Latin America and the Caribbean (OPANAL).

The Treaty was signed on 14 February 1967, at Tlatelolco, a borough of Mexico City. The basic obligation of the parties to the Treaty, defined in article 1, is to use exclusively for peaceful purposes the nuclear material and facilities under their jurisdiction, and to prohibit and prevent in their respective territories the very presence of nuclear weapons for any purpose and under any circumstances. Parties to the Treaty also undertake to refrain from engaging in, encouraging or authorizing, directly or indirectly, or in any way participating in the testing, use, manufacture, production, possession or control of any nuclear weapons.

Annexed to the Treaty are two Additional Protocols, which create a system of obligations for extra-continental and continental States having responsibility *de jure* or *de facto* for territories in the zone of application of the Treaty as well as obligations for the nuclear-weapon States. Thus, under Additional Protocol I, France, the Netherlands, the United Kingdom and the United States would agree to guarantee nuclear-weapon-free status to those territories for which they are, *de jure* or *de facto*, internationally responsible. The Protocol has been signed and ratified by the Netherlands, the United Kingdom and the United States. France has signed it and has declared that it will in due course take an appropriate decision, considering that not all States concerned in the zone are yet parties to this Treaty. Under Additional Protocol II, nuclear-weapon States pledge to respect fully the "denuclearization of Latin America in respect of warlike purposes" and "not to use or threaten to use nuclear weapons against the Contracting Parties". By 1979, all five nuclear-weapon States had adhered to it, and in that connection made individual declarations with respect to various provisions of the Treaty and its Protocols.[6]

As at June 1990, the Treaty was in force for 23 Latin American States that had ratified it and had waived the requirements for entering into force set out in article 28 (that all States in the zone be parties to the Treaty, that all States to which the Protocols apply adhere to them and that relevant safeguards agreements be concluded with IAEA). Several States within the denuclearized zone are not yet parties to the Treaty, among them Cuba, which has not signed the Treaty. Argentina has signed but has not ratified it, and Brazil and Chile have ratified it but not waived the requirements for its entry into force. Argentina, as a signatory, has officially declared that it would not act against the objectives of the Treaty.

c.
Various proposals

The discussion of the question of establishing nuclear-weapon-free zones in various parts of the world is continuing between regional States concerned and within the United Nations disarmament bodies. While supporting the concept as such, many Member States stress the importance of certain prerequisites for the successful implementation of the concept of nuclear-weapon-free zones. Among the principles and objectives most referred to are the following: the initiative should come from the States in the region concerned and the arrangements to establish a nuclear-weapon-free zone should be based on agreement freely arrived at among the States of the prospective zone; the arrangements should take into account the specific characteristics of the region in question; such arrangements should contain provisions concerning verification of the commitments undertaken; the nuclear-weapon States should undertake obligations to respect the status of the denuclearized zone and not to use or threaten to use nuclear weapons against the States of the zone. In addition, some States judge proposals for such zones also from the standpoint of their potential contribution not only to the security of the region concerned, but to international security in general.

For many years, debates have taken place in the General Assembly on the possibility of setting up nuclear-weapon-free zones in Africa,[7] the Middle East[8] and South Asia.[9] In addition, there have been proposals for the creation of such zones in other regions, including Northern Europe, Central Europe, the Balkans and South-East Asia. Some exploratory work has been carried out both at the regional and international level on these possibilities. However, no concrete negotiations have yet been initiated on any of these proposals. Although there has been considerable support for some proposals, not all of them have received support by all countries concerned.

C.
Limitation on stationing of nuclear weapons

Setting geographical limitations on the stationing of nuclear weapons is an approach to reducing the nuclear threat. Although there is no prohibition on deployment of nuclear weapons on the high seas, some States would like to have the seas used exclusively for peaceful and non-nuclear purposes. Others point to their rights to free navigation of the seas in customary law and under the United Nations Convention on the Law of the Sea. The agreements concluded so far in this respect, unlike nuclear-weapon-free zones, largely cover unpopulated territories on the Earth and in outer space. In one instance, the scope is also broader since it provides not only for denuclearization, but also demilitarization of the area.

1.
The Antarctic Treaty

The Antarctic Treaty, concluded on 1 December 1959, was the first international agreement that, by establishing a demilitarized zone, *ipso facto* provided that nuclear weapons would not be introduced into a specified area. The Treaty bans "any measures of a military nature" such as the establishment of military bases and fortifications, military manoeuvres and the testing of any type of weapon. This was the first Treaty to provide for on-site inspection. The Treaty entered into force on 23 June 1961 and the number of parties to it has increased from the original 12 signatories in 1959 to 39 as at the end of 1989, including the five nuclear-weapon States.

2.
Outer Space Treaty

The Treaty on Principles Governing the Activities of States in the Exploration and Use of Outer Space, including the Moon and Other Celestial Bodies (Outer Space Treaty) (resolution 2222 (XXI), annex), was opened for signature on 27 January 1967 and entered into force on 10 October the same year. As at 31 December 1989, 91 States had become parties to the Treaty.

The Treaty prohibits the placing in orbit around the Earth of any objects carrying nuclear weapons or any other kinds of weapons of mass destruction, installing such weapons on celestial bodies or stationing them in outer space in any other manner. The Treaty also affirms that the Moon and other celestial bodies are to be used exclusively for peaceful purposes and that the establishment of military bases, installations and fortifications, the testing of any type of weapons and the conduct of military manoeuvres on celestial bodies are to be prohibited.

A further instrument, the Agreement Governing the Activities of States on the Moon and Other Celestial Bodies, was concluded in 1979. It entered into force on 11 July 1984. By the end of 1989, seven countries (Australia, Austria, Chile, Netherlands, Pakistan, Philippines and Uruguay) had become parties to it. It complements the Outer Space Treaty and prohibits the use of force on the Moon, the placing of any weapons, including nuclear weapons, on or in orbit around it, or any kind of militarization of it or other celestial bodies.

3.
Sea-Bed Treaty

The Treaty on the Prohibition of the Emplacement of Nuclear Weapons and Other Weapons of Mass Destruction on the Sea-Bed and the Ocean Floor and in the Subsoil Thereof (Sea-Bed Treaty) (resolution 2660 (XXV), annex) was opened for signature on 11 February 1971. It entered into force on 18 May 1972. By the end of December 1989, 82 States had ratified the Treaty while 23 States had signed it but not yet ratified it.

The Treaty provides that the States parties to it undertake not to place on or under the sea-bed, beyond the outer limit of a 12-mile coastal zone, any nuclear weapons or any other weapons of mass destruction or any facilities for such weapons. All parties have the right to verify through observation activities of other States in the area covered by the Treaty.

Three Review Conferences of the parties to the Treaty have been held so far, in 1977, 1983 and 1989. At all three Review Conferences, the parties reaffirmed their commitment to the Treaty. In addition, at the general debate at the Third Conference, the Soviet Union, the United Kingdom and the United States for the first time declared that they "have not emplaced any nuclear weapons or other weapons of mass destruction on the sea-bed outside the zone of application of the Treaty as defined by its article II and have no intention to do so".[10]

D.
Limitations and reductions of nuclear weapons

There have been a number of efforts to limit and reduce the stockpiles of nuclear weapons in the world. While the consideration of these issues took place both within the United Nations and the Conference on Disarmament, where nuclear disarmament is viewed as a priority item on their respective agendas, the actual negotiations on a number of specific measures were pursued in bilateral negotiations between the United States and the Soviet Union. In the process, these two nuclear-weapon Powers have concluded several agreements providing for quantitative limitations and some qualitative restrictions on their nuclear forces.

During the 1970s the bilateral negotiations between the Soviet Union and the United States were carried out within the framework of the so-called strategic arms limitation talks (SALT), which resulted in the signing of several specific agreements. The negotiations continued in the early 1980s under the new name of the strategic arms reduction talks (START). In their joint statement of January 1985, the two sides defined their subject as a complex of questions concerning space and nuclear weapons, both strategic and intermediate/medium-range, with all the questions to be considered and resolved in their interrelationships. The statement also pointed out that "ultimately the forthcoming negotiations, just as efforts in general to limit and reduce arms, should lead to the complete elimination of nuclear arms everywhere".[11]

Under the general umbrella entitled nuclear and space talks (NST), the negotiations have been conducted in three different groups assigned to deal respectively with strategic nuclear weapons, intermediate/medium-range nuclear weapons, and defence and space issues. In the course of those negotiations, a great deal of progress has been achieved.

1.
INF Treaty

A most significant result of bilateral efforts was achieved in 1987 with the conclusion of the Treaty between the United States of America and the Union of Soviet Socialist Republics on the Elimination of their Intermediate-Range and Shorter-Range Missiles (INF Treaty).[12] The Treaty is notable because it provides, for the first time, for the complete elimination of an entire class of American and Soviet nuclear missiles and because it contains unprecedented intrusive verification provisions. It was signed in Washington by President Reagan and General Secretary Gorbachev on 7 December 1987 and came into force on 1 June 1988. The Treaty is of unlimited duration.

In the preamble, the parties expressed their conviction that the measures set forth in the Treaty would help to reduce the risk of an outbreak of war. They also recalled their obligations under article VI of the Treaty on the Non-Proliferation of Nuclear Weapons, namely to pursue negotiations in good faith on effective measures for the cessation of the nuclear-arms race at an early date.

The basic obligation of the two parties consists of an undertaking to eliminate their intermediate-range and shorter-range missiles, together with their launchers, all support structures and support equipment. Intermediate-range missiles (1,000–5,500 km) would be eliminated not later than three years after the entry into force of the Treaty, while the elimination of shorter-range missiles (500–1,000 km) would be completed not later than 18 months after the Treaty's entry into force. The Protocol on Elimination provides that the nuclear warheads and guidance elements may be removed from the missiles, prior to their elimination, and retained by the deploying country.

The verification system of the Treaty provides, *inter alia*, for on-site inspection and inspection on short notice, and provides for non-interference with national technical means of verification. The on-site inspection covers the main facility of each side where components for missiles are being produced, i.e. the Votkinsk Machine Building Plant in the Soviet Union and the Hercules Plant in Utah in the United States. While intermediate-range missiles are prohibited, the Votkinsk plant also produces another type of missile that is also monitored. After two years of monitoring at both plants, if no such missiles are produced for 12 months, the monitoring portals will be removed and may not be replaced. Inspection on short notice applies to all specified sites other than production facilities. The inspectors are to be allowed to carry out such inspections not only during the initial three-year period envisaged for complete elimination of these weapons, but also during the next 10 years, thus extending the duration of the whole arrangement to 13 years altogether. Furthermore, the actual removal of the weapons covered by the Treaty from deployment areas and storage is subject to verification. Besides missile installations on American and Soviet soil, this includes American and Soviet missile bases in Western and Eastern Europe.[13] Occasional inspection of the locations will take place also over a 13-year period.

Following the conclusion of the INF Treaty, the Warsaw Treaty States proposed in April 1989 negotiations on tactical nuclear arms in Europe (see A/44/228). Those States were convinced that along with the elimination of the intermediate-range and shorter-range missiles, the phased reduction and eventual elimination of the tactical nuclear arms in Europe would help to lessen the danger of war, strengthen confidence and establish a more stable situation on the continent. This would, in their opinion, facilitate progress towards deep cuts in strategic nuclear arms and, ultimately, the complete elimination of nuclear weapons everywhere.

The member States of NATO, in their report entitled "A Comprehensive Concept of Arms Control and Disarmament" adopted at the NATO summit meeting in May 1989 (A/44/481, annex II), declared that once implementation of an agreement on conventional force reductions in Europe was under way, the United States, in consultation with the allies concerned, was prepared to enter into negotiations to achieve a partial reduction of American and Soviet land-based nuclear missile forces of shorter range to equal and verifiable levels. In April 1990, NATO agreed that negotiations on tactical nuclear weapons could start after the conclusion of an agreement on conventional force reductions in Europe.[14] Pursuant to NATO decisions taken in 1979 and 1983, the United States unilaterally withdrew 35 per cent, i.e. 2,400, of its nuclear weapons based in Western Europe. The Soviet Union, in the course of 1989, also unilaterally withdrew 500 tactical nuclear warheads from the territory of its allies. The Soviet Union furthermore declared that it was prepared to withdraw during 1989–1991 all nuclear ammunition from the territories of its allies on the condition of a similar reciprocal step on the part of the United States. In June 1990, the Soviet Union announced that by the end of 1990 it would unilaterally reduce in the European region 140 short-range missile launchers as well as 3,200 pieces of nuclear artillery and 1,500 nuclear charges.

2.
Strategic arms reduction talks

The United States and the Soviet Union are in the process of finalizing an agreement on substantial reductions of their strategic nuclear arsenals, the so-called START agreement. In June 1990, Presidents Bush and Gorbachev on the occasion of their summit meeting at Washington issued a joint statement outlining the basic provisions of the future treaty. The two sides will translate the agreed outline into specific treaty language. It is their declared intention to complete this work within months.

The Treaty would provide for both sides to carry out up to 50 per cent reductions in certain categories of strategic offensive arms. The Treaty would also include a reduction in the overall number of warheads deployed on delivery vehicles (ICBMs, SLBMs, heavy bombers) to no more than 6,000. The aggregate throw-weight of the deployed ICBMs and SLBMs of each side will be limited to 50 per cent below the present level of the Soviet Union. Heavy bombers equipped for long-range nuclear ALCMs will be counted as one delivery vehicle against the 1,600 limit and shall be attributed with an agreed number of warheads against the 6,000 limit. Existing and future United States heavy bombers equipped for long-range nuclear ALCMs will be attributed with 10 warheads each. Existing and future Soviet heavy bombers equipped for long-range nuclear ALCMs will be attributed with eight warheads each.

The Treaty will also include specific prohibitions on certain categories of strategic offensive arms, basing modes and activities. The following items would be banned: new types of heavy ICBMs; heavy SLBMs and launchers for heavy SLBMs; mobile launchers for heavy ICBMs; new types of ICBMs and SLBMs with more than 10 re-entry vehicles; flight testing and deployment of existing types of ICBMs or SLBMs with a number of re-entry vehicles greater than the number specified in the Washington Summit Joint Statement of December 1987; rapid reload of ICBM launchers; long-range nuclear ALCMs equipped with multiple independently targetable warheads. Sea-launched cruise missiles (SLCMs) will not be constrained in the START treaty. On the other hand, each side will provide the other with unilateral, politically binding declarations regarding its planned deployment of nuclear SLCMs with a range over 600 km. The maximum number of deployed SLCMs for each of the following five treaty years will not exceed 880 for each side.

The verification régime for the reductions and other constraints to be contained in the treaty would include on-site inspections; national technical means of verification; a ban on denial of telemetric information; data-information exchange on numbers, locations and technical characteristics of strategic arms and an agreement on the manner of deployment of mobile ICBMs and limitations on their movements so as to ensure effective verification. A joint compliance and inspection commission will be established to promote the objectives of the treaty. The treaty would have a duration of 15 years with the possibility of extension for successive five-year periods.

3.
Strategic arms limitation talks

Although new arrangements on strategic armaments, most notably the forthcoming START treaty, would go much farther than previous treaties, the strategic arms limitation talks (SALT) between the United States and the Soviet Union in the 1970s have played an important role in the efforts of the two sides to place certain limitations on the development of their nuclear-weapon arsenals.

Thus, by the Interim Agreement between the United States of America and the Union of Soviet Socialist Republics on certain measures with respect to the limitation of strategic offensive arms (SALT I),[15] with a Protocol attached, the two sides undertook not to start construction of additional fixed land-based ballistic missile launchers and to limit submarine missile launchers and modern ballistic missile submarines to an agreed level for each side. The limits agreed upon allowed, however, for an additional increase in the total number of the strategic forces of the two sides. However, the SALT II agreement, signed in June 1979, set totals not only on missiles, but also on sub-category totals. The ceilings agreed upon went quite a way towards dealing with the very different needs of the United States, which had most of its warheads on submarines in the form of SLBMs, and the Soviet Union, which had most of its strategic assets in ICBM silos. It brought the long-range bomber forces into the calculations and even considered the new technology of air-launched cruise missiles (ALCMs). It did not reduce the number of warheads either side had, or restrict the use of any existing technology, but it did restrict major new technological developments and set some predictability in the strategic selection. It also served to work out many definitions and issues that were carried over into subsequent negotiations, such as START.[16] Although the SALT II Treaty[17] has not been formally ratified, both parties have in general observed the limitations set by it. These limitations will, however, be largely superseded by the terms envisaged under the START agreement.

Another important agreement concluded in the framework of SALT negotiations was the 1972 Treaty Between the United States of America and the Union of Soviet Socialist Republics on the Limitation of Anti-Ballistic Missile Systems (ABM Treaty),[18] subsequently amended by a Protocol of 3 July 1974. By the ABM Treaty, the Soviet Union and the United States undertook not to develop, test or deploy mobile land- or sea-based, air- or space-based ABM systems. They also agreed to limit ABM systems to two sites with no more than 100 launchers at each site. In 1974, the Treaty was amended by a Protocol that limited each side to one ABM deployment area only. The Soviet Union chose to maintain its ABM system in the area centred on its capital, Moscow, and the United States chose to maintain its system in the ICBM deployment area in North Dakota. Subsequently, the United States decided not to deploy its ABM system at all.

The ABM Treaty received considerable attention in the bilateral negotiations following the announcement of the United States strategic defense initiative (SDI) in 1983 (see chap. III, sect. D). The Soviet Union took the position that the provisions of the ABM Treaty prohibited all testing of ballistic missile defence systems and their components in outer space. For its part, the United States has maintained the position that the SDI research programme is not incompatible with the ABM Treaty.

Besides different interpretations of the relationship between SDI and the ABM Treaty, the Soviet Union and the United States disagreed on the effect that such a programme, if and when fully developed, might have on the strategic balance between the two sides. The United States views it as an entirely defensive programme with no effect on START, while the Soviet Union held the view that the programme if implemented would deny it second strike retaliatory capability, the preservation of which for both sides constitutes the essence of the ABM Treaty. In September 1989, the Soviet Union expressed its willingness to sign and to ratify the START treaty without waiting for the completion of bilateral discussions of the ABM problem. At the same time, it proceeds from the assumption that both sides will continue to comply with the existing ABM Treaty as signed, and that its violation by any side would automatically relieve the other side from its obligations under the START treaty. The United States and the Soviet Union have also declared their commitment to work towards early and effective agreements aimed at preventing an arms race in space and terminating it on Earth.

The question of outer space first became the subject of bilateral negotiations between the United States and the Soviet Union in the 1970s. The initial discussions took place from 1977 to 1979 and focused on the question of anti-satellite activities. In August 1983, the Soviet Union proposed to the United States to ban ASAT systems and to eliminate existing ones, but the United States did not agree to this proposal. The new bilateral negotiations began in 1985 as part of the nuclear and space talks (NST), which also included START and INF as separate negotiations. At the Washington summit meeting in May/June 1990, both sides agreed to continue negotiations on ABM and space within the negotiating framework of NST.

E.
Limitation on testing of nuclear explosive devices

Since nuclear testing is an inherent part of the process of development of nuclear weapons, many States have given highest priority to a comprehensive nuclear-test ban (CTB), i.e. a prohibition of all tests, in all environments. They point out that such a ban would introduce uncertainties in the qualitative development of nuclear weapons that would make the development of these weapons more difficult; that it would also largely prevent the acquisition of nuclear weapons by States that do not have them; and that it would therefore contribute to the goal of nuclear non-proliferation. Nuclear-weapon States, with the exception of the Soviet Union, are not prepared to accept a nuclear-test ban, because they assess nuclear testing as essential for the credibility, reliability and survivability of their nuclear deterrent forces. The United States has stated that a CTB remains a long-term United States objective and that such a ban must be viewed in the context of a time when the United States no longer needs to depend on nuclear deterrence to ensure international security and stability, and when it has achieved broad, deep and verifiable arms reductions, greatly improved verification capabilities, expanded confidence-building measures and greater balance in conventional forces.

In 1963 the Soviet Union, the United Kingdom and the United States concluded a Treaty Banning Nuclear Weapon Tests in the Atmosphere, in Outer Space and Under Water.[19] The Treaty was negotiated in response to environmental and other concerns being expressed at the time. It does not prohibit underground tests provided they do not cause radioactive debris to be present outside the territory of the State where the test was conducted. In its preamble, however, it notes the objective of achieving "the discontinuance of all test explosions of nuclear weapons for all time". The Treaty has since been joined by many other States and had, as at June 1990, 118 parties. Two nuclear-weapon States, France and China, are not parties, although they announced, in 1974 and 1986 respectively, that their future tests would be carried out only underground.[20] France has stated that it is not prepared to enter any comprehensive test-ban agreement, although President Mitterrand has recently indicated that France would not be the last to stop testing. China stated that it was flexible towards the creation of the subsidiary body in the Conference on Disarmament on the issue. It also stated that if and when an agreement was reached on a mandate enabling such a body to be established, it would participate in its work.[21]

In 1974, the United States and the Soviet Union signed the so-called Threshold Test Ban Treaty (TTBT), which prohibits all weapon tests with a yield exceeding 150 kilotons. Because it is impossible to distinguish nuclear-weapons tests from nuclear explosions for peaceful purposes, in 1976, both States also signed the Peaceful Nuclear Explosions Treaty (PNET),[22] which puts a 150-kiloton limit on such explosions. Difficulties arose in connection with verification procedures for both Treaties and, therefore, neither Treaty was ratified. In 1987, the United States and the Soviet Union agreed to a step-by-step approach to the objective of the ultimate cessation of all testing and in that context initiated negotiations on improved verification procedures for those Treaties. Following the successful conclusion of those negotiations, during the Washington summit meeting in May/June 1990, the Soviet Union and the United States signed verification protocols for both Treaties, which will pave the way for their ratification by the respective legislative bodies of the two countries.

International efforts to achieve a complete test ban began in the 1950s. From 1977 to 1980, three nuclear-weapon States, the Soviet Union, the United Kingdom and the United States, held negotiations on a comprehensive test ban without reaching final agreement. The Conference on Disarmament at Geneva was periodically informed on the progress of these trilateral negotiations.

Most States have taken the position that the step-by-step approach agreed on by the United States and the Soviet Union is insufficient because it does not specify when a comprehensive ban is to be achieved. They continue to call for an immediate ban on all testing. At the United Nations, General Assembly resolutions attaching the highest priority to the conclusion of a comprehensive nuclear-test ban have been voted on and adopted by an overwhelming majority. The Conference on Disarmament has been requested by the Assembly in successive years to begin negotiations on such a treaty. Some States have submitted draft treaties and different proposals on this subject to the Conference on Disarmament, but no negotiations have been initiated. Given their position on the issue, most nuclear-weapon States remain opposed to the commencement of multilateral negotiations towards a CTBT in the Conference on Disarmament. At the same time, they have stated their readiness to discuss issues related to such a ban on a non-negotiating basis.

Recently, some States parties to the PTBT have proposed amending the Treaty into a comprehensive test ban. In accordance with the amendment procedure provided for in the Treaty, any amendment requires the consent of all three original parties.[23] A meeting for the organization of the conference was held from 29 May to 8 June 1990 and adopted a number of organizational decisions. The Amendment Conference is scheduled to be held at New York from 7 to 18 January 1991, although two of the original parties, the United States and the United Kingdom, have already stated that they will oppose the proposed amendment.

Stating that it would uphold the idea of a CTB and that it wishes to promote it by practical steps, the Soviet Union held a unilateral moratorium on nuclear tests for 18 months in 1985–1987. No other nuclear-weapon State followed the Soviet Union's move.

As noted before, bans on testing have also been included in the two nuclear-weapon-free zone Treaties. The Treaty of Tlatelolco prohibits weapons testing in Latin America and the Caribbean. In view of their expressed concerns about nuclear weaponry and about the possible environmental effects of testing, the parties to the Treaty of Rarotonga undertook to prevent the testing of any nuclear explosive device in their territories and throughout the zone, and not to assist or encourage the testing of any such device by any State.

The verification aspects of a comprehensive test ban have received considerable attention. A variety of means, including satellite data and radiation monitoring, have allowed the international community to verify adherence to the ban on atmospheric tests. Underground testing has traditionally been monitored using seismic techniques although other techniques have been devised as a complement. Efforts are being made in the Conference on Disarmament to design a global seismic network for acquisition and exchange of data. Many believe that seismic monitoring, backed up by other methods, could detect and identify tests down to very low yields (1–2 kilotons) and that this testing threshold would impose severe constraints on nuclear-weapons development. However, there is some concern that no verification system would be able to detect sub-kiloton explosions.

The verification arrangements agreed upon in the verification protocols to the TTBT and the PNET, signed at the Washington summit meeting in May/June 1990, include hydrodynamic yield measurement (the so-called CORRTEX method), on-site inspection and seismic monitoring on the territory of the testing party as well as national technical means.

F.
Constraints on the use of nuclear weapons

Over the years, many initiatives have been put forward concerning the prohibition or limitation of the use of nuclear weapons. In the process, various approaches developed on this issue. They ranged from the calls for unconditional prohibition of the use of nuclear weapons to prohibition of first use and various conditional bans. After the conclusion of the 1968 Treaty on the Non-Proliferation of Nuclear Weapons, the question of adequate security assurances to non-nuclear-weapon States against the use of nuclear weapons emerged. Such guarantees were also contemplated within the framework of the establishment of nuclear-weapon-free zones in various regions of the world. Still another approach dealt with the limitation of the use of nuclear weapons from the point of view of customary norms of international humanitarian law in conventional wars as the basis for deriving some principles applicable to nuclear weapons as well. The question of the prohibition of the use of nuclear weapons was also considered within the broader question of the prevention of war, in particular nuclear war. This approach gained prominence especially during the 1980s.

No tangible progress has been made towards the conclusion of an agreement regarding the non-use of nuclear weapons. Many nations have expressed the hope that the depth and scope of changes presently taking place in international relations, particularly between the two major nuclear-weapon States, have considerably diminished the likelihood of their possible deliberate use.

The main thrust of various approaches to this issue, particularly those pursued in the last decade, are described briefly below.

1.
Consideration in the General Assembly

The General Assembly has passed a great number of resolutions on this subject. With the exception of procedural resolutions, all resolutions have been adopted by vote. The voting has shown deeply rooted divergencies, reflecting different strategic doctrines and national security perceptions.

The question of the use of nuclear weapons received a great deal of attention at the 1978 special session of the General Assembly devoted to disarmament in a broader context of the elimination of the danger of war. At that session, the five nuclear-weapon States made individual declarations with regard to security assurances to non-nuclear-weapon States.[24]

At the second special session of the General Assembly devoted to disarmament, in 1982, various suggestions and proposals were put forward. The Soviet Union, for instance, declared that, with immediate effect, it assumed an obligation not to be the first to use nuclear weapons, because it believed that should a nuclear war start it could mean the destruction of humankind. A similar statement already had been made by China in 1964 when it exploded its first atomic weapon.

The United Kingdom, also at the second special session on disarmament, stated that it was its long-established policy that nuclear weapons should never be used except in self-defence under most extreme circumstances.[25]

In the consideration of the issue, the United States and other Western countries pointed out that a declaration on the non-first use of nuclear weapons would restrict and undermine the wider principle of self-defence enshrined in the Charter of the United Nations. They noted that the Charter provided that States refrain from the threat or use of force in their international relations (Art. 2.4) but that it did not impair the inherent right of individual or collective self-defence if an armed attack occurs (Art. 51), and it did not contain any prohibition of any specific means of warfare.

At its thirty-seventh session and subsequently, in resolutions initiated by Argentina, the German Democratic Republic and India, the General Assembly, respectively recommended that the Conference on Disarmament undertake negotiations on: appropriate and practical measures that could be negotiated and adopted individually for the prevention of nuclear war;[26] an international instrument of a legally binding character laying down the obligation not to be the first to use nuclear weapons;[27] and an international convention prohibiting the use or threat of use of nuclear weapons under any circumstances, taking as a basis the text of a draft convention annexed to it.[28]

2.
Actions and statements outside the United Nations

In 1984, for the first time, the Conference on Disarmament included in its agenda a separate item entitled "Prevention of nuclear war, including all related matters". While all members recognized the importance of the prevention of nuclear war, there remained differences in approach between various groups. Eastern European and non-aligned States, believing that the removal of the threat of nuclear war was the most urgent task, urged the Conference to undertake, as a matter of highest priority, negotiations on measures for the prevention of nuclear war and to establish an *ad hoc* committee for that purpose. For their part, Western countries maintained that the question of preventing nuclear war could not be isolated from the problem of preventing war in general and that the question at issue was how to maintain peace and international security in the nuclear age. As a result of these differences in approach, matters related to the non-use of nuclear weapons and prevention of nuclear war have continued until now to be considered only in plenary meetings of the Conference.

The question of constraints on the use of nuclear weapons and the prevention of nuclear war was also addressed on several occasions by various world leaders. Their statements have made an impact on the deliberations and negotiations in various forums.

For instance, the joint message of 24 October 1985 by the Heads of State or Government of six countries — Argentina, Greece, India, Mexico, Sweden and the United Republic of Tanzania — (the so-called "Six-Nation Initiative") directed to the leaders of the United States and the Soviet Union in connection with their summit meeting stated that "since the citizens of all nations are equally threatened by the consequences of nuclear war, it is of utmost importance to us also that your meeting should create appropriate conditions and produce concrete steps towards disarmament and peace" (A/40/825-S/17596, annex).

The United States-Soviet joint statement issued on 21 November 1985 on the occasion of the summit meeting between President Reagan and General Secretary Gorbachev stated that the two leaders, conscious of the special responsibilities of their respective countries for maintaining peace, "have agreed that a nuclear war cannot be won and must never be fought" (A/40/1070, annex). Furthermore, "they emphasized the importance of preventing any war between them, whether nuclear or conventional" and stated that they would not seek to achieve military superiority. In the joint statement issued at Washington on 10 December 1987 (A/43/58, annex) following their signing of the INF Treaty, President Reagan and General Secretary Gorbachev affirmed the fundamental importance of their meetings at Geneva (1985) and Reykjavik (1986), which had laid the basis for concrete steps in a process intended "to improve strategic stability and reduce the risk of conflict".

In February 1988, the six nations issued the Stockholm Declaration, in which they welcomed the signing of the INF Treaty (A/43/125-S/19478, annex). They viewed it as a "historic first step" and as significant evidence that "a reversal is possible". They also pointed out that no nation had the right to use nuclear weapons and declared that "what is morally wrong should also be explicitly prohibited by international law through a binding international agreement".

At the special ministerial meeting of the Non-Aligned Countries held at Havana in May 1988, the Final Communiqué stated (A/S-15/27, annex, para. 18):

> "The Ministers emphasized that, pending the attainment of general and complete disarmament — a process in which nuclear disarmament plays a central role — it was necessary for nuclear-weapon States, *inter alia*, immediately to negotiate an agreement on the prohibition of the use or the threat of use of nuclear weapons and to pledge not to be the first to use them. The Ministers further urged that non-nuclear-weapon States be given assurances against the threat or use of nuclear weapons by any nuclear-weapon State."

The Declaration issued at the Conference of Heads of State or Government of Non-Aligned Countries at Belgrade in September 1989 (see A/44/551-S/20870, annex) said:

> "The USSR and the USA have, for the first time in history, signed a treaty to eliminate some of the existing nuclear weapons. The Heads of State or Government welcomed this step and reiterated their expectation that it would be a precursor to the adoption of concrete disarmament measures leading to the complete elimination of nuclear weapons."

3.
Security assurances

The question of security assurances to non-nuclear-weapon States was first raised specifically in connection with the negotiations on the 1968 Treaty on the Non-Proliferation of Nuclear Weapons (NPT).

In order to provide a counterbalance to the undertaking of the non-nuclear-weapon States not to acquire nuclear weapons, as embodied in the Non-Proliferation Treaty, three nuclear-weapon States — the Soviet Union, the United Kingdom and the United States — agreed to provide certain security assurances to these countries through a Security Council resolution.

Security Council resolution 255 (1968) recognized that aggression with nuclear weapons, or the threat thereof, against a non-nuclear-weapon State party to the Treaty would call for immediate action by the Council and, above all, by its nuclear-weapon States permanent members. The Council also welcomed the intention expressed by certain States to assist any non-nuclear-weapon State party to the Non-Proliferation Treaty that was a victim of an act or threat of nuclear aggression and reaffirmed the right to collective self-defence under Article 51 of the Charter of the United Nations.

However, a number of non-nuclear-weapon States, while welcoming the "positive" assurance provided for in the resolution, expressed preference for "negative" assurance, i.e. a commitment by nuclear-weapon States that they would not use or threaten to use nuclear weapons against non-nuclear-weapon States. All five nuclear-weapon States have provided unilateral negative security assurances, although those assurances reflect the different security perceptions of the nuclear-weapon States.[29]

The question has been actively considered by the Conference on Disarmament. Each year since 1979, with only one exception, 1986, the Conference on Disarmament has established *ad hoc* working bodies on effective international arrangements to assure non-nuclear-weapon States against the use or threat of use of nuclear weapons. Although there has been no objection in principle to the idea of an international convention, the difficulties involved as regards developing a "common formula" on the substance of security assurances, which would be acceptable to all States, have also been pointed out.

In recent years, the search for a common formula in the *ad hoc* committee on the nature and scope of security assurances has focused on the consideration of various new ideas put forward on the understanding that an agreement on the substance of the arrangements would facilitate the agreement on their form. Two basic approaches have been examined at the Conference on Disarmament negotiations — the single common formula and the "categorizational approach". The former seeks to find one common formula of security assurances covering all non-nuclear-weapon States which are to be assured. The latter envisages that a specific common formula should be developed for each category of non-nuclear-weapon States, which, in order to take into account the diversity of their security situations, are categorized along the lines of certain criteria (such as non-nuclear status, non-stationing of nuclear weapons, alliance status) as already reflected in the unilateral declarations of the nuclear-weapon States. The idea of following a step-by-step approach has also been advanced, with the understanding that, when viewed in a broader perspective, the two basic approaches could complement each other. Various views on the suggested approaches have been expressed at the negotiations in the Conference on Disarmament and their consideration remains inconclusive.[30] In November 1989, Nigeria submitted for consideration by the States parties to the Non-Proliferation Treaty a proposal for an agreement on the prohibition of the use or threat of use of nuclear weapons against non-nuclear-weapon States parties to that Treaty. The proposal was also submitted to the Conference on Disarmament in March 1990, and to the Fourth NPT Review Conference.[31]

G.
Confidence-building measures

The general goal of these measures is to reduce and possibly eliminate causes for mistrust, misunderstanding and fear, all of which contribute to instability and insecurity. There is need for confidence-building in many fields — political, military, economic and social, among others. Traditional security concerns, mainly military, have been, however, the main source of confidence-building measures (CBMs). Where confidence already exists, CBMs are a way to reinforce it, but they are no substitute for arms regulation and disarmament measures as such.

Regarding CBMs specifically concerned with various aspects of nuclear weapons, wide-ranging efforts have been promoted by nuclear-weapon States, most notably the United States and the Soviet Union, but also France and the United Kingdom. Most of the agreements in this field were concluded in the 1960s and 1970s and were related to the process of the strategic arms limitation talks.[32]

Thus, in September 1987, the two sides concluded an Agreement on the Establishment of Nuclear Risk Reduction Centres.[33] According to the Agreement, each party shall establish in its capital a national nuclear risk reduction centre (NRRC). The parties shall use the centres to transmit the following types of notifications: notifications of ballistic missile launches under article IV of the Agreement on Measures to Reduce the Risk of Outbreak of Nuclear War between the USSR and the United States of 1 September 1971; notifications of ballistic missile launches under paragraph 1 of article VI of the Agreement between the USSR and the United States on the Prevention of Incidents on and over the High Seas of 25 May 1972; other communications that each party may, at its own discretion as a display of good will and with a view to building confidence, transmit to the other party. In May 1988, the Soviet Union and the United States signed an Agreement on Notifications of Launches of ICBMs and SLBMs. According to that

Agreement, each party agreed to provide the other party notification, through the nuclear risk reduction centres, no less than 24 hours in advance, of the planned date, launch area and area of impact for any launch of an ICBM or SLBM.[34]

In June 1989, they signed an Agreement on the Prevention of Dangerous Military Activities, reflecting the desire of the two States to reduce the risk of outbreak of nuclear war, in particular as a result of misinterpretation, miscalculation or accident.[35] The accord, which took effect on 1 January 1990, covers four areas of possible conflict:

a.   an agreement to refrain from the use of force in the event of a border incursion by the other nation's military forces, aircraft or ships;

b.   an agreement not to use laser-range finders or other like devices while the two sides' forces are in close proximity. These devices can temporarily blind soldiers if they are struck directly in the eye;

c.   an agreement to set up "special caution zones" in areas such as the Persian Gulf, when both sides' forces come into contact; and

d.   an agreement to refrain from electronic jamming of either side's command and communications systems.

It is also envisioned that direct communications between the nations' military units in the field will be established to prevent misunderstandings. At the Wyoming ministerial meeting, held in September 1989, both sides signed an agreement on advance notification of major strategic exercises. Under this agreement, each side must provide the other side, on a reciprocal basis, with no less than 14 days' advance notification of the commencement of the one large-scale strategic exercise, with the participation of heavy bombers, which it intends to conduct in the course of each calendar year. At the Washington summit meeting, in May/June 1990, the Soviet Union and the United States agreed to pursue new talks with the objective of reducing further the risk of outbreak of war, particularly nuclear war, and of ensuring strategic stability, transparency and predictability.

H.
Nuclear weapons and international law

Despite wide-ranging discussions in various forums, no uniform view has emerged as yet on the legal aspects of the possession of nuclear weapons and their use as a means of warfare.

The Charter of the United Nations, a document signed just before the world entered the nuclear era, does not refer to the existence of nuclear weapons. The Charter states, in Article 51, that "nothing ... shall impair the inherent right of individual or collective self-defence if an armed attack occurs against a Member of the United Nations". Under the circumstances, the question of which means are acceptable for exercising the right of self-defence if an attack occurs is left to treaty regulations and to customary law.

Some countries, including nuclear-weapon States, consider that nothing in the existing treaty practice of States or in international customary law could be construed to apply to the question of the legality of nuclear weapons either directly or indirectly. Furthermore, they take the position that the use of these weapons is the subject of the decision of the national authorities of the country concerned, which is based on the considerations of its national security requirements and, when applicable, the specific commitments explicitly undertaken in that regard, such as those envisaged in connection with nuclear-weapon-free zones.

On the other hand, many countries believe that norms and emerging norms relating to the legality of nuclear weapons and their use derive from a variety of existing sources. In this connection, they point out that the Statute of the International Court of Justice indicates as sources of international law, besides treaties, also "international custom, as evidence of a general practice law" and "the general principles of law recognized by civilized nations". It is thus argued that in dealing with the question of the regulation of the possession and the use of nuclear weapons, the guiding principles could be drawn not only from specific treaty provisions, but also from international customary law, general principles of law, judicial decisions and, in some cases, from the resolutions of the Security Council.[36]

The proponents of this approach, for instance, point out that customary norms of international humanitarian law applicable in armed conflicts contain some general principles that could be considered to impose certain constraints on the use not only of conventional, but also of nuclear weapons. In their view, the well-established principle in the law of armed conflicts that "the right of the Parties to the conflict to choose methods or means of warfare is not unlimited"[37] is particularly relevant. They also maintain that there are many other principles of international customary law that have in fact been reflected in modern treaty practice.[38]

In this context, they usually refer to the following:

a.   a ban on means or methods of warfare that cause unnecessary suffering (in relation to the military objectives that the belligerents hope to attain);

b.   the requirement of distinction (between military targets on the one hand and the civilian population and its property on the other);

c.   a ban on warfare that leads to indiscriminate effects (weapons or methods of warfare that strike at random against military and civilian values);

d.   proportionality (excessive civilian losses when compared with the concrete and direct military advantage to be expected from the attack).

Although those principles largely overlap, at the same time, in the opinion of their proponents, their implications are far-reaching. Thus, for instance, the principle of distinction, that both a civilian population and civilian objects as such must not become the target of an armed attack, would imply that "counter-value" strikes would not be allowed. Likewise, the principle of indiscriminate effects means that nuclear attacks that would lead inexorably to massive civilian losses must be avoided. From the principle of proportionality, they infer that nuclear weapons may not as a rule be used in densely populated areas.

It is, however, not clear in juridical theory how the existing customary law could be applied with regard to the regulation of the production and possession of such weapons. It is argued in this connection that for a norm to have the status of international customary law, it must reflect a general perception of the norm as legally binding (an *opinio juris*) and be shown to prevail among the members of the international community. Although there are other views on this question, the fact remains that no consensus (or "near consensus") and thus no general *opinio juris* has emerged on the question of the production and possession of nuclear weapons.

Notes

1.   For details, see NPT/CONF.III/64/1.

2.   See *United Nations Disarmament Yearbook*, vol. 10, 1985 (United Nations publication, Sales No. E.86.IX.7), appendix VII.

3.   The positions of the nuclear-weapon States are described in the Memorandum from the Secretariat of the South Pacific Forum on the Subject of the South Pacific Nuclear-Free Zone Treaty Prepared for the Fourth Review Conference of the Parties to the Treaty on the Non-Proliferation of Nuclear Weapons (NPT/CONF.IV/16).

4.   See *Official Records of the General Assembly, Fifteenth Special Session, Plenary Meetings*, A/S-15/PV.4. Foreign Minister Roland Dumas, in his statement at the third special session of the United Nations on disarmament, said:

> "That leads to the question of what we customarily refer to as denuclearized zones. My country has always favoured the establishment of such zones. Naturally, any such undertaking must flow from the unanimous decision of all the States concerned and must be subject to satisfactory control. Moreover, their creation must be military and geographically relevant.

> "Clearly, therefore, where nuclear deterrence operates directly, it would be artificial and would add nothing to security to designate regions and declare them denuclearized. It is in the name of these same principles that France has refused to ratify the Protocols of the Rarotonga Treaty instituting a nuclear-free zone in the South Pacific.

> "The unanimous consent of States? How could one credit that, when plainly the Treaty in question is aimed at one of the States in the region which conducts its nuclear tests there?

> "Geographically relevant? This condition is unfulfilled also, given the ambiguities of the Treaty terms concerning navigation and ports of call. If it jeopardizes freedom of navigation, denuclearization can never be legitimate.

> "Militarily relevant? This, too, is dubious, in view of the total absence of any risk of nuclear proliferation in the zone concerned."

5.   United Nations, *Treaty Series*, vol. 634, No. 9068.

6.   *Status of Multilateral Arms Regulation and Disarmament Agreements*, 3rd edition, 1987 (United Nations publication, Sales No. E.88.IX.5).

7.   The resolutions were adopted with the following voting results: 40/89 A (148-0-6); 41/55 A (150-0-5); 42/34 A (151-0-4); 43/71 A (151-0-4); and 44/113 A (147-0-4).

8.   Since 1980 all resolutions were adopted without a vote.

9.   The resolutions were adopted with the following voting results: 40/83 (104-3-41); 41/49 (107-3-41); 42/29 (114-3-36); 43/66 (116-3-34); and 44/109 (116-3-32).

10.   See document SBJ/CONF.III/15, para. 13.

11.   Conference on Disarmament documents CD/570 and CD/571.

12.   "Summary and text of the INF Treaty and Protocols", in *Arms Control Today*, vol. 18, No. 1 (January-February 1988), supplement, pp. 1-16. *The United Nations Disarmament Yearbook*, vol. 12, 1987 (United Nations publication, Sales No. E.88.IX.2), appendix VII.

13.   It covers bases in the following States: Belgium, Czechoslovakia, German Democratic Republic, Germany, Federal Republic of, Italy, Netherlands and United Kingdom.

14.   *Arms Control Today*, May 1990, p. 27.

15.   United Nations, *Treaty Series*, vol. 944, No. 13445, p. 3.

16.   The important details of SALT II can be summarized as follows: (a) an equal ceiling of 2,400 on the parties' aggregate of ICBMs, SLBMs and heavy bombers; (b) an equal sub-ceiling of 1,320 on any one of the three categories; (c) an equal sub-ceiling of 1,200 on launchers for MIRVed ICMBs and SLBMs; and (d) an equal sub-ceiling of 820 on MIRVed ICBMs. The different sets of limits are to allow each side to vary its force mixes, which would be legitimate as long as they did not breach any one of the ceilings and sub-ceilings.

17. Treaty between the USA and the USSR on the Limitation of Strategic Offensive Arms (see CD/53/Appendix III/vol. I, document CD/28).

18. United Nations, *Treaty Series*, vol. 944, No. 13446.

19. United Nations, *Treaty Series*, vol. 480, No. 6964, p. 43.

20. See *The United Nations Disarmament Yearbook*, vol. 13, 1988 (United Nations publication, Sales No. E.89.IX.5), p. 201.

21. *Official Records of the General Assembly, Forty-fourth Session, Supplement No. 27* (A/44/27), p. 19.

22. For the text of the Treaty, see *Arms Control and Disarmament Agreements*, United States Arms Control and Disarmament Agency, Washington, D.C., 1982.

23. For details, see NPT/CONF.IV/2.

24. For updated versions of the individual declarations, see NPT/CONF.IV/11.

25. *Official Records of the General Assembly, Tenth Special Session, Plenary Meetings*, A/S-10/PV.14.

26. The resolutions were adopted with the following voting results: 37/78 I (130-0-17); 38/183 G (128-0-20); 39/148 P (128-6-12); 40/152 Q (136-3-14); 41/86 G (134-3-14); 42/42 D (140-3-14); and 43/78 F (136-3-14).

27. The resolutions were adopted with the following voting results: 37/78 J (112-19-15); 38/183 B (110-19-15); 39/148 D (101-19-17); 40/152 A (123-19-7); 41/86 B (118-17-10); 42/42 A (125-17-12); 43/78 B (127-17-6); and 44/119 B (129-17-7).

28. The resolutions were adopted with the following voting results: 37/100 C (117-17-8); 38/73 G (126-17-6); 39/63 H (128-17-5); 40/151 F (126-17-6); 41/60 F (132-17-4); 42/39 C (135-17-4); 43/76 E (133-17-4); and 44/117 C (134- 17-4).

29. *The United Nations Disarmament Yearbook*, vol. 14, 1989, (United Nations publication, Sales No. E.90.IX.4), chap. VIII, annex.

30. For details, see *Official Records of the General Assembly, Forty-fourth Session, Supplement No. 27* (A/44/27).

31. NPT/CONF.IV/17.

32. Memorandum of Understanding Regarding the Establishment of a Direct Communications Link (1963); Agreement on Measures to Improve the United States-USSR Direct Communications Link (1971); Agreement on Measures to Reduce the Risk of Outbreak of Nuclear War (1971); Agreement on the Prevention of Nuclear War (1973); and Agreement on the Prevention of Incidents on and over the High Seas (1972). The Soviet Union concluded almost identical agreements on the prevention of high-sea incidents with the United Kingdom in 1986, the Federal Republic of Germany in 1988, and with Canada, France, Italy and Norway in 1989.

33. CD/814 and CD/815.

34. CD/845 and CD/847.

35. CD/943.

36. Burns H. Weston, "Nuclear weapons versus international law: 'contextual reassessment'", *McGill Law Journal*, vol. 28, No. 3, July 1983, p. 541.

37. Quotation from art. 35 (1), Protocol I, of the 1977 Additional Protocols to the Geneva Conventions of 1949.

38. *Ibid.*, art. 35 (2). Additional Protocol I at present has 92 parties. Among the nuclear-weapon States, China and the Soviet Union have ratified the Protocol and the United Kingdom is expected to do so.

IX
Conclusions

Nuclear weapons represent a historically new form of weaponry with unparalleled destructive potential. A single large nuclear weapon could release explosive power comparable to all the energy released from the conventional weapons used in all past wars.

Only two nuclear weapons have ever been used in a war. Today, there are about 50,000 nuclear warheads in the possession of the nuclear-weapon States. The quantitative growth of the nuclear-weapon arsenals has, however, been stopped. The number of nuclear warheads is now declining.

In recent years, there has been a marked improvement in the overall international political climate and in relations between a number of States in various regions of the world. The most far-reaching changes have taken place in Europe, a continent where the two major nuclear Powers and their military alliances have confronted each other for decades. New political patterns are emerging there, whereby long-standing differences are being resolved and the cold war is ending. Although tensions remain in some other regions, several fierce armed conflicts have been brought to an end and the process of peacefully resolving some other conflicts has been initiated. The United Nations has played an important role in the process of conflict-resolution and peace-keeping and thereby made a tangible contribution to the maintenance of international peace and security, one of its main objectives.

These positive developments in the world, in particular the *rapprochement* between East and West, have given strong impetus to arms limitation and disarmament efforts, especially in Europe.

The most tangible results thus far have been achieved in the bilateral negotiations between the United States and the Soviet Union. In December 1987, the Soviet Union and the United States concluded the first agreement in history — the INF Treaty — which provides for the destruction of a whole category of nuclear missiles, and as such represents a major breakthrough in the disarmament process. In terms of quantitative reductions of strategic nuclear weapons, significant progress has been made in bilateral START negotiations between the United States and the Soviet Union. The framework of an agreement signed at Washington in June 1990 at the summit meeting between President Bush and President Gorbachev provides for a drastic cut in various categories of their strategic offensive arms. Their agreement to continue negotiations on further cuts and effective limitations on qualitative improvements in both strategic and tactical nuclear weapons is most important.

The United States and the Soviet Union have stated that reducing the risk of outbreak of nuclear war is the responsibility not only of the United States and the Soviet Union, but that other States should also make their contribution toward the attainment of this objective.

East and West are expected to reach an agreement on significant reductions of conventional forces in Europe that would facilitate additional cuts of other nuclear weapons stationed in Europe. In addition, several countries in both East and West — including the Soviet Union and the United States — are now unilaterally taking steps to reduce and to restructure their military forces.

Notwithstanding the bilateral agreements between the United States and the Soviet Union concerning nuclear weapons, their nuclear stockpiles will continue to be far in excess of those of the other nuclear-weapon States for the foreseeable future.

Qualitative improvements of nuclear weapons have continued. Nuclear tests are still carried out, though at a reduced rate. The production of fissionable material for weapons purposes has been reduced.

Most countries in the world consider that an early end to nuclear testing by all States in all environments would be an essential step towards preventing the qualitative improvement and the development of new nuclear weapons and would also contribute to the goal of non-proliferation. Most nuclear-weapon States consider that their reliance on nuclear weapons for their security requires their continued testing and do not agree that a comprehensive test ban is an urgent necessity.

The United States and the Soviet Union have agreed to continue to co-operate in the field of monitoring nuclear-weapon tests. Multilateral and bilateral efforts to perfect verification methods for a comprehensive nuclear-test ban are important for achieving the ultimate complete cessation of such tests.

In the 1980s, the deployment of nuclear weapons at sea also became the subject of growing attention of many States. About 30 per cent of nuclear weapons are earmarked for maritime deployment. Sea-borne strategic nuclear weapons are subject to bilateral negotiations between the United States and the Soviet Union. This is not yet the case with regard to non-strategic sea-based nuclear weapons intended for targets at sea and on land.

Another feature of the 1980s has been the preoccupation of many non-nuclear-weapon States with the question of legal restraints on nuclear weapons, particularly as regards their non-use. Considering that, since 1945, no single nuclear weapon has actually been used, they believe that the *de facto* non-use of nuclear weapons might eventually serve as the basis for establishing a customary norm on the non-use of nuclear weapons. They believe that the different approaches to international customary and treaty law that relate to this matter deserve further consideration. Some nuclear-weapon States do not agree with this assessment.

There is a manifest conviction of the entire international community that a major nuclear war would have catastrophic consequences for the whole world. During the last decade, the nuclear Powers have clearly stated their determination to avoid any nuclear conflict. This was most convincingly expressed both in the 1985 solemn declaration by President Reagan and General Secretary Gorbachev that "a nuclear war cannot be won and must never be fought" and in the statement by President Mitterrand that "nuclear weapons are weapons of non-use".

The Heads of State and Government of the North Atlantic Alliance confirmed on 6 July 1990 that they would "never in any circumstance be the first to use force", and announced that in a transformed Europe the Allies concerned would be able to adopt a new strategy making nuclear forces truly weapons of last resort.

In the last decade, the findings of several scientific studies about the possible effects of nuclear war, including the climatic effects subsumed in the concept of "nuclear winter", have added a new dimension to the discussion of the global consequences of nuclear war. These studies, *inter alia*, suggested that a nuclear war might cause more casualties than previously thought in countries other than those immediately involved.

The Chernobyl reactor accident in 1986, though not comparable to a nuclear detonation because it was only the source of radioactive debris and did not have the other effects peculiar to a nuclear explosion, provided a concrete demonstration of the magnitude of the consequences of even a relatively limited release of radioactive matter.

During the 1980s, the question of the contamination of the environment in connection with military and civilian nuclear activities, and the effects of such contamination, received increased public attention. In this regard, the work being done by the relevant national and international organizations is valuable in helping to understand the impact of these activities on health and the environment.

The momentous changes in the world, particularly in the East-West relationship, have diminished the threat of nuclear confrontation and made it possible to start a real process of reduction of nuclear weapons. The United States and the Soviet Union are engaged in far-reaching bilateral negotiations, which they have agreed should ultimately lead to the complete elimination of nuclear arms everywhere. Other nuclear-weapon Powers have stated that they would be willing to take part in the process of nuclear disarmament at an appropriate stage. Moreover, as recently reiterated by the Disarmament Commission, all States have the right and the duty to be concerned with and to contribute to efforts in the field of disarmament.

However, differences remain between States concerning mainly the timing and procedures for nuclear disarmament measures, on the one hand, and the existence and scope of international norms regarding nuclear weapons, on the other.

The nuclear non-proliferation régime is as important as ever. Its strict observance is of continued fundamental importance. Concern about nuclear proliferation remains acute, particularly in the light of technological developments that could make the acquisition of nuclear weapons by additional States easier, and in the light of the uncertainties surrounding the policies of some States, including some involved in regional rivalries and tensions.

Further efforts are necessary to prevent the acquisition or manufacture of nuclear weapons by additional States, to strengthen the international non-proliferation régime and to achieve wider participation in it. The régime would also be strengthened if NPT parties that have not already done so concluded the requisite safeguard agreements with IAEA.

The right of States to develop nuclear technology for economic benefit must be reconciled with the need to ensure against the further spread of nuclear weapons. Prior to any transfer of fissionable materials, nuclear equipment or know-how, acceptance of appropriate IAEA safeguards is an especially important part of the agreement between supplier and recipient.

To achieve the objectives of non-proliferation of nuclear weapons, global and regional efforts are needed, including those aimed at further strengthening the non-proliferation régime in all its aspects.

International security is now being perceived on the basis that reliance on military strength for national security will be increasingly supplemented by policies of confidence-building and wide co-operation in various fields, and negotiation and dialogue with the view to strengthening the security of all.

Official doctrinal positions of the nuclear-weapon States

China

Basic positions of the Government of China on nuclear weapons and nuclear disarmament

1.   China has consistently opposed the arms race and is dedicated to the cause of maintaining world peace and security. China always stands for disarmament and complete prohibition and thorough destruction of nuclear weapons.

2.   China declared on the very first day when it came into possession of nuclear weapons that at no time and under no circumstances would it be the first to use nuclear weapons. China respects the status of the existing nuclear-weapon-free zones and will not use, or threaten to use, nuclear weapons against non-nuclear-weapon States or nuclear-weapon-free zones.

3.   With respect to nuclear disarmament, China is of the view that:

    a.   The ultimate goal of nuclear disarmament should be the complete prohibition and thorough destruction of nuclear weapons. All measures aimed at nuclear disarmament should serve the realization of this goal;

    b.   The United States of America and the Union of Soviet Socialist Republics possess the world's largest and most sophisticated nuclear arsenals and are still improving and upgrading their nuclear weapons. They bear a special responsibility for halting the nuclear arms race and reducing nuclear weapons. They should take the lead in halting the testing, production and deployment of all types of nuclear weapons, reducing and destroying drastically all types of nuclear weapons that they have deployed anywhere inside or outside their countries. After this is done, a broadly representative international conference on nuclear disarmament may be convened with the participation of all nuclear-weapon States to discuss further steps and measures for thorough destruction of nuclear weapons. This would be a truly effective way to achieve nuclear disarmament;

      c.   As an effective measure to prevent nuclear war, all nuclear-weapon States should undertake not to be the first to use nuclear weapons at any time and under any circumstances, and not to use or threaten to use nuclear weapons against non-nuclear-weapon States and nuclear-weapon-free zones. On this basis, an international convention banning the use of nuclear weapons should be concluded with the participation of all the nuclear-weapon States.

France
Defence doctrine of France

1.   France's defence doctrine rests on nuclear deterrence. As the President of the Republic said in his speech to the Institute of Advanced National Defence Studies on 11 October 1988:

"Deterrence means preventing any possible aggressor from meddling with our vital interests because of the risks he would run. Deterrence does not exist to win war but to prevent, to forestall it."

2.   The point is that the weak can deter the strong by means of a range of resources capable of persuading the opponent that the nuclear risk he runs on his own territory would outweigh any benefit he might think to gain by attacking France.

3.   A nuclear weapon is thus a political weapon, a diplomatic weapon for keeping balance and countering blackmail from any source. It renders the very enterprise of war pointless, since war becomes impossible to win.

4.   This is why France's deterrent force does not seek to match the opponent's nuclear capacity but is based on the idea of sufficiency, made possible by the equalizing power of the atom.

5.   This is also why it must be maintained above the credibility threshold by means of continuous, technologically wholly independent modernization.

6.   Given the seriousness of the stakes, France considers that only a threat to its vital interests — that is, the very existence of the nation — could justify the use of its *force de frappe* (strike force). For that very reason, the decision to use force rests with the Head of State alone, whose autonomy must be absolute: he is the one who has to define where France's vital interests begin.

7.   French deterrence has another component, the final warning, which is an integral part of it. The final warning, delivered against a military target — by pre-strategic weapons in the first instance, even if the final warning is not solely a matter for short-range weapons — is to indicate to the aggressor that the vital interests of France are at stake and that continued aggression will result in strategic weapons being used.

8.   By offering a chance of last-minute negotiations, the final warning theory enhances overall deterrence.

9.   France's autonomy of decision allows the criteria for and timing of the use of nuclear force in the event of aggression to remain uncertain, thus increasing the deterrence effect.

10.   While nuclear weapons, on which deterrence rests, have been chiefly responsible for keeping the peace for more than 40 years, and while France believes that the human mind cannot come up with any credible alternative to nuclear weaponry for exercising deterrence, this of course does not make France any less well-disposed towards efforts to reduce nuclear over-armament. It thus attaches the highest priority to Soviet-American strategic talks and devoutly hopes for an agreement resulting in a substantial reduction in the arsenals concerned. It hopes that those efforts will continue.

11.   The French President, speaking on 28 September 1983 at the United Nations, clearly stated the three prior conditions France has set before it will take part in any negotiations:

"The first of these conditions is the correction of the fundamental difference, in terms of type and quantity, between the armaments of the two major Powers and those of the others ...

"The second condition flows from the wide gap between conventional forces, particularly in Europe, a gap which has become even wider ... because of the existence of chemical and biological weapons, the manufacture and stockpiling of which must be prohibited by a convention.

"The third condition is the cessation of the escalation in anti-missile, anti-submarine and anti-satellite weapons."

12.   France devoutly hopes that these conditions will be fulfilled and will spare no effort to attain this end.

Union of Soviet Socialist Republics
Military doctrine of the USSR

    1.   Soviet military doctrine is profoundly defensive, aimed at guaranteeing the security of the USSR and its allies. Its goal is not to prepare for, but to prevent, nuclear war.

    2.   That goal was reflected, in particular, in the Soviet Union's pledge never in any circumstances to be the first to use nuclear weapons. That most important political act reflects the determination of the Soviet Union to work for the gradual reduction and, ultimately, complete elimination of the risk of a nuclear war. The Soviet Union believes that a nuclear war must never be fought and cannot be won.

    3.   The Soviet Union is a staunch opponent of war in all its aspects. It considers that a nuclear war, once begun, would assume global proportions and would have disastrous consequences not only for the belligerents but for all mankind; the assumption that such a war can be restricted to one region or theatre of operations is untenable.

    4.   Historically, the Soviet Union was compelled to develop nuclear weapons and subsequently assemble nuclear forces as a countermeasure.

    5.   However, the USSR considers that state of affairs to be an intermediate stage in the radical reduction of nuclear weapons — which has already begun — since the current balance of the nuclear potentials of the opposing sides is disproportionately high and, for the time being, only guarantees equal peril for both sides. The continuation of the nuclear-arms race will inevitably increase that equal peril and may lead to a situation in which even parity will cease to be a factor in military and political restraint.

    6.   Hence, the Soviet Union is in favour of guaranteeing strategic stability at the lowest possible level of nuclear balance and, in the long run, eliminating nuclear weapons completely. This goal, of course, cannot be achieved immediately. It has to be approached through a process of step-by-step reductions by all nuclear-weapon States, with guarantees, at every stage, of international security and strategic stability.

    7.   The Soviet Union has put forward a balanced programme for the elimination of nuclear weapons by the year 2000, which was presented in the statement by the General Secretary of the Central Committee of the Communist Party of the Soviet Union, Mr. M. S. Gorbachev, on 15 January 1986.

United Kingdom of Great Britain and Northern Ireland
United Kingdom nuclear doctrine: Deterrence after the INF Treaty

1. The central aim of the NATO Alliance's defence effort is clear and simple: to remove the option of war permanently from the East/West scene. Nuclear weapons have made this aim wholly compelling and for that very reason wholly attainable. Their virtually infinite destructive power has made nonsense of the idea of war as a contest of strength. That result is irreversible, since it rests on scientific knowledge that cannot be forgotten. The right course is not to attempt vainly to dissolve it, but to build around it a war-prevention system that, without surrendering the great stability we have now, will become progressively less costly and less abrasive.

2. The goal must be a system giving each side thorough assurance — grounded, amid the strains of a changing world, not on beliefs about attitude or motive but on objective military fact — that the other neither has nor seeks options for resolving differences by force. If the East shares that goal, it can increasingly be attained through open and well-understood policies cancelling war not through the brandishing of armaments but through their quiet maintenance at the lowest level needed to ensure that the utter irrationality of aggression remains a plain certainty.

3. Much that President Gorbachev has said encourages us to hope that he may see the central security need increasingly as we do. There seems ground for optimism that, both in the extensive arms control agenda and elsewhere, he will be ready to work with us towards a less tense and costly security system. The Soviet Union still has much larger forces in most categories, and its strategic situation is not the same as the West's; its priorities therefore are different. But with agreement on the central goal, patient and clear-sighted work can bring both parties steadily closer to it in safety.

4. The 1987 INF Treaty, achieved as growing Soviet realism converged with NATO steadfastness, was a major advance in easing tension and building confidence. Its content was specific and exact: the strictly verified abolition of a defined class of missiles. Nothing in it implies an agreement to abandon operational roles or strategies, or leave a hole in the middle of NATO's ability to respond flexibly.

5. Flexible response is the only strategic concept that makes sense for a defensive alliance in the nuclear age. Military victory in

the classical sense is not feasible; the use of force at any level, but especially the nuclear level, can have no other aim than to deny an aggressor swift success and to show him that he has underrated the defender's resolve and must, for his own survival, back off. The circumstances in which this task would arise could vary greatly; the defence must therefore have a wide range of options, enabling it to react to any military situation promptly and with the least force needed for the basic political aim of ending the war. Nothing in the INF Treaty makes this strategy less apt than before, or reduces the need to ensure, through the manifest ability to implement it in credible ways, that aggression can never be attractive.

6. For flexible response NATO has to maintain an effective nuclear armoury at several levels. Strategic weapons alone, for all their awesome power, could not be morally tolerable, practically feasible or politically credible for every scenario. Our needs at non-strategic levels will continue to evolve in line with our arms-control commitments, with new technology and with deeper understanding on both sides of the minimum imperatives of mutually assured security. NATO has made major cuts in its non-strategic armoury; the number of warheads in Europe is now 35 per cent less than in 1979, and will fall further by mid-1991. The INF Treaty's abolition of intermediate-range missiles follows past NATO decisions to abandon successively nuclear infantry weapons, nuclear anti-aircraft missiles and nuclear land-mines.

7. Cuts in the armoury can go further yet, and the alliance is working on the possibilities. But the aim for which the armoury as a whole exists, of surely preventing war, cannot be served if we attempt to follow simultaneously both the path of cuts and the path of obsolescence. Nuclear weapons are not mere symbols; like other weapons, they can deter only by evident capability for effective use. Modern technology offers major improvements in range, accuracy and target-acquisition, and these can enable us to cut weapon numbers. But there is no prudent basis for making the cuts without the improvements.

8. NATO is studying how to keep up-to-date its armoury of warheads supported by the provision of delivery systems and basing arrangements in which European nations rightly share the burden. NATO's military authorities have reported on this to the Nuclear Planning Group. Ministers will consider the steps that need to be

taken, for example, replacing the Lance missile, to keep the armoury as a whole at the standard of effectiveness and versatility, and no larger than the minimum size, needed to sustain its purpose.

9.   The United Kingdom will continue to play a full part in this effort, and also to maintain the independent non-strategic contribution without which the value of our strategic force, which provides a separate second centre of nuclear decision-making in support of Alliance strategy, would be seriously incomplete. Our non-strategic contribution has since the 1960s rested on WE177 free-fall weapons, usable from various aircraft and in various roles. For technical and operational reasons, these cannot all be relied upon beyond the 1990s. As with the rest of the Western armoury, numbers and types may not have to be kept at present levels; that needs further study. But, under the strategy of flexible response, the basic need for some non-strategic weapons will remain, and procurement lead-times means that initial decisions on modernization — particularly on the choice of an air-launched missile to which warhead work at Aldermaston will be geared — must be taken before long.

10.   Work like this has its full counterpart on the Soviet side. Nothing that President Gorbachev has said or done is ground for imagining that he will run military risks with his country's security on suppositions about Western goodwill. We must be similarly objective, recognizing that if there is indeed a Soviet reassessment enabling us all to work together more constructively, it would be folly to dismantle, or let decay, the very structures that have helped to induce it. Cool and steady realism of this kind is not an obstacle but the best guide to strengthening the security system we seek — one in which the total neutralization of war, by agreed non-confrontational means, becomes so sure, accepted and permanent that, even when interests may differ widely, nations of East and West can conduct their business together by means in which the thought of armed conflict simply plays no part.

United States of America
United States deterrence policy

1.   Deterrence works by making clear that the costs of aggression will exceed any possible gain. This is the basis of United States military strategy against both conventional and nuclear aggression; because conflict carries the risk of escalation, the United States goal

is to dissuade aggression of any kind and to prevent coercion of the United States, its allies and friends.

2.   To ensure deterrence, the United States must make clear that it has both the capability and the will to respond effectively to coercion or aggression. While emphasizing its resolve to respond, the United States must avoid specifying just what form the response will take. This is the essence of "flexible response", which has been United States policy since 1961 and a key element of NATO strategy since 1967. A potential aggressor faces three types of possible response by the United States:

   a.   Direct defence: to pose the possibility that aggression will be stopped without actions that escalate the conflict. This is sometimes referred to as "deterrence through denial". Defending against conventional attack with conventional forces is an example of direct defence;

   b.   Threat of escalation: to warn that aggression could start hostilities that might not be confined to conventional response only, and that escalation could lead to costs that far outweigh any possible gain and that are greater than an aggressor anticipates or could bear. In this regard, NATO's deterrence of aggression is enhanced by NATO resolve to use nuclear weapons, if necessary, to halt that aggression;

   c.   Threat of retaliation: to raise the prospect that an attack will trigger a retaliatory attack on the aggressor's homeland, causing him losses that far outweigh any possible gain.

3.   While deterrence requires capabilities across the entire spectrum of nuclear conflict, its essential foundation is provided by United States strategic nuclear forces and the doctrine that supports them. The United States must ensure that the effectiveness of these forces and the will to use them, if necessary, are never in doubt.

4.   The United States maintains diversified strategic retaliatory forces to prevent a disarming first strike. It maintains a variety of basing modes, launch platforms and attack vehicles, with a triad of submarine-launched ballistic missiles, ground-based intercontinental ballistic missiles and strategic bombers. Adequate and survivable command, control and communications are also essential to United States force structure and to the credibility of the deterrent.

5.   United States forces and targeting policy must be perceived as making nuclear warfare unacceptable. The United States does not target populations as an objective in itself and seeks to minimize collateral damage through more accurate, lower-yield weapons.

6.   Holding at risk the full range of a potential aggressor's assets is necessary for deterrence, but is not sufficient. United States options in response to aggression cannot be limited to capitulation or mutual destruction. The United States must have the capability and the resolve to employ a broad range of military options.

7.   Finally, the United States requires residual capability, as leverage for early war termination and to avoid post-conflict coercion. For this reason, a nuclear reserve force is an integral part of United States strategic forces. In addition, the United States maintains continuity of government programmes to ensure its capability to retaliate in case of an attack aimed at incapacitating its political and military leadership.

8.   These capabilities do not imply that the United States seeks the ability to fight a nuclear war. The United States has repeatedly emphasized that nuclear war cannot be won and must never be fought. But any adversaries must understand that they cannot gain their objectives through nuclear warfare or nuclear coercion under any circumstances.

9.   Continuing modernization of United States forces is essential. While the United States is committed to arms reductions as one component of policy for enhancing United States and allied security, this does not remove the need for modern nuclear forces for deterrence. Neglecting modernization in expectation of arms reduction agreements would decrease the likelihood of such agreements by reducing incentives to negotiate.

Land- and sea-based nuclear weapons

Weapon type	Number in service	Range (km)	Warhead load and yield	Warhead type	Number in the stockpile
1.					
United States[a]					
ICBMs					
Minuteman II	450	11 300	1 × 1.2 Mt	W56	450
Minuteman III	200	13 000	3 × 170 kt	W62	600
Minuteman III (MK12A)	300	13 000	3 × 335 kt	W78	900
MX	50	11 000	10 × 300 kt	W87	500
	1 000				2 450
SLBMs					
Poseidon	224	4 600	10 × 40 kt	W68	2 240
Trident I	384	7 400	8 × 100 kt	W76	3 072
	608				5 312
Bombers					
B-1B	97	9 800	22 total either ALCM (200 kt each, 2,500 km) or bombs (B28, 61, 83) or SRAM		1 614
FB-111A	59	4 700	6 SRAM (170 kt, 200 km) or 6 bombs (B43, 61, 83)		2 484
B-52G/H	193	16 000	B-52G/H 20 SRAM or B-52G 12 ALCMs and 6 bombs; B-52H 12 ALCM externally mounted and 8 internally mounted		1 140
	349				5 238

B-1Bs and B-52s can carry a mix of 8 weapons mounted externally and 24 weapons in internal bomb racks. The FB-111A can carry 6 weapons, excluding ALCMs, B53 and B28. Individual bombs in the United States inventory can vary greatly in yield. The B28 has 5 yields, 4 of which are known: 70 kt, 350 kt, 1.1 Mt and 1.45 Mt. The B43 has a 1 Mt yield. The B53 has a 9 Mt yield. The B57 has a sub 20 kt yield. The B61-0, -1, -7 have 4 yield options in the 100-500 kt range. The B83 is said to have a yield of 1,000+ kt. The W69 Short-Range Attack Missile (SRAM) has a yield in the 170-200 kt range, and the W80-1 Air-Launched Cruise Missile (ALCM) has a 200-250 kt yield.[b]

Weapon type	Number in service	Range (km)	Warhead load and yield	Warhead type	Number in the stockpile
Land-based aircraft[c]	2 250	1 060-2 400			1 800
F-4 C/D/E			2,170 lbs. max. 3 × bombs (B28RE, B43, B57, B61, B83 Genie)		
F-15 A/C			5 pylons 16,000 lbs. max. (W25, 833 lbs. each or Genie 1.5 kt)		
F-16 A/B/C/D			possibly 5 nuclear weapons (B43, B57)		
F-111 A/D/E/F			3 bombs (B43, B57, B61, B83)		
Missiles					
Pershing II	111	1 790	1 × .3-80 kt	W85	125
GLCM	250	2 500	1 × .2-150 kt	W84	325

Land- and sea-based nuclear weapons [*continued*]

Weapon type	Number in service	Range (km)	Warhead load and yield	Warhead type	Number in the stockpile
Pershing IA	72	740	1 × 60-400 kt	W50	100
Lance	100	125	1 × 1-100 kt	W70	1 282
Nike Hercules	27	160	1 × 1-20 kt	W31	75
					1 907

Artillery

155 mm and 203 mm	3 850	30	1 × .1-12 kt		1 540
Atomic Demolition Munition (ADM)	150	..	1 × .01-1 kt	W54	150

Naval systems

Carrier aircraft 1450	1 100^d				
A-6E			3 × B28 or B43 or B57 or B61, also Harpoon		
A-7E			4 × (B28, B43, 57, 61)		
F/A-18A/B			2 × (B61)		

Marine Corps

A-4M			1 × (B28, 43, 57, 61)		
AV-6B			1 × B61		

ASW systems

ASROC	?	1-10	1 × 5-10 kt	W44	574
SUBROC	?	60	1 × 5-10 kt	W55	285
ASW aircraft	710	1 160-3 800	1 × <20 kt	B57	897

Aircraft include P-3A/B/C, S-3A/B, SH-3D/H. Some of the B57 nuclear depth bombs are allocated to British Nimrods, Italian Atlantics and Dutch P-3s.

Missiles

Tomahawk (land attack)	200	2 500	1 × 5-150 kt	W80-0	200

Naval SAMs

Terrier	?	35	1 × 1 kt	W45	290^e

2.
Soviet Union

ICBMs

SS-11 Mod 2		13 000	1 × .950-1.1 Mt		160
Mod 3	380	10 600	3 × 100-350 kt (MRV)		630
SS-13 Mod 2	60	9 400	1 × 600-750 kt		60
SS-17 Mod 2	110	10 000	4 × 750 kt (MIRV)		480
SS-18 Mod 4	308	11 000	10 × 550 kt (MIRV)		3 080
SS-19 Mod 3	320	10 000	6 × 500 kt (MIRV)		2 100
SS-24	58	10 000	10 × 100 kt (MIRV)		200
SS-25	162	10 500	1 × 550 kt		150
	1 398				6 860

SLBMs

SS-N-6 Mod 3	240	3 000	2 × .375-1 Mt (MRV)		480
SS-N-8 Mod 1/2	286	7 800	1 × 1-1.5 Mt		286
SS-N-17	12	3 900	1 × .5-1 Mt		12
SS-N-18 Mod 1/3		6 500	7 × 200-500 kt		
Mod 2	224	8 000	1 × .45-1 Mt		1 568
SS-N-20	100	8 300	10 × 100 kt		1 000
·SS-N-23	80	7 240	4 × 100 kt		256
	942				3 602

Land- and sea-based nuclear weapons [*continued*]

Weapon type	Number in service	Range (km)	Warhead load and yield	Warhead type	Number in the stockpile
Bombers					
Tu-95 A		8 300	4 bombs		30
Tu-95 B/C		8 300	5 bombs or AS-3		100
Tu-95 G		8 300	4 bombs and 2 AS-4		270
Tu-95 H	153	8 300	8 AS-15 and 4 bombs		600
Tu-160 Blackjack	9	?	AS-15 and 4 bombs		100
	162ᶠ				1 100
Anti-ballistic missiles					
ABM-1B (Galosh)	32	320	1 × unknown		32
ABM-3	68	70	1 × low yield		68
	100				100ᵍ
Land-based systems					
Aircraft					
Tu-26	180	4 000	1-3 × bombs or ASM		360
Tu-16	210	3 100	1-2 × bombs or ASM		250
Tu-22	330	2 900-3 300	1-2 × bombs or 1 ASM		120
Tactical aircraft	4 050	700-1 300	1-2 × bombs		3 230
Missiles					
SS-20	318	5 000	3 × 250 kt		1 215
SS-4	18	2 000	1 × 1 Mt		65
SS-12	135	900	1 × 500 kt		405
SS-1c	620	280	1 × 1-10 kt		1 370
SS-23	239	500	1 × 100 kt		239
FROG7	658	70	1 × 1-25 kt		200
SS-21	289	120	1 × 10-100 kt		1 100
SS-SHCH Scud b	601	?	?		?
SS-C-1b	100	450	1 × 50-200 kt		100
SAMs	7 000	40-300	1 × low yield		4 000
Artillery	6 760	10-30	1 × low yield		2 000
ADMs	?	?	?		?
Naval systems					
SS-N-5	36	1 400	1 × 1 Mt		36
Aircraft					
Tu-26	140	4 000	1-3 × bombs or ASM		280
Tu-16	170	3 100	1-2 × bombs or ASM		170
Tu-22	30	2 900-3 300	1 × bombs		30
ASW aircraft	375	...	1 × depth bombs		400

Nuclear-capable tactical aircraft include MiG-21 Fishbed L, MiG-23 Flogger B/G, MiG-27 Flogger D/J, Su-7B Fitter A, Su-17 Fitter C/D/H and Su-24 A/B/C/D/E.
ASW aircraft include Be-12 Mail, Il-38 May, Tu-142 Bear F, Ka-25 Hormone and KA-27 Helix helicopters.

Weapon type	Number in service	Range (km)	Warhead load and yield	Warhead type	Number in the stockpile
Anti-shipping missiles					
SS-N-3	228	450	1 × 350 kt		120
SS-N-7	90	65	1 × 200 kt		44
SS-N-9	208	280	1 × 200 kt		78
SS-N-12	200	550	1 × 350 kt		76
SS-N-19	136	550	1 × 500 kt		56
SS-N-22	80	100	1 × 200 kt		24

Land- and sea-based nuclear weapons [*continued*]

Weapon type	Number in service	Range (km)	Warhead load and yield	Warhead type	Number in the stockpile
Land attack					
SS-N-21	4	3 000	1 × 200 kt		16
SS-NX-24	0	<3 000	1 × ?		0
ASW missiles/torpedoes					
SS-N-15		37	1 × 10 kt		?
SS-N-16	400	120	1 × 10 kt		400
Fras-1	25	30	1 × 5 kt		25
Torpedoes type	65	16	1 × low kt		
ET-80	575	>16	1 × low kt		575
Naval SAMs					
SA-N-1	65	22	1 × 10 kt		
SA-N-3	43	37	1 × 10 kt		
SA-N-6	33	65	1 × kt		260[h]

3.
United Kingdom

Aircraft					
Buccaneer S2B	25	1 700	1 × 5-400/200 bomb	WE177	
Tornado GR-1	220	1 300	1-2 × 400/200 kt	WE177	155-175
SLBMs					
Polaris A3-TK (Chevaline)	64	4 700	2 × 40 kt	MRV	128
Carrier aircraft					
Sea Harrier FRS 1	42	450	1 × 10 kt	WE177	42
ASW helicopters					
Sea King HAS 5	56	...	1 × 10 kt		
Lynx HAS 2/3	78	...	1 × 10 kt		25[i]

4.
France

Aircraft					
Mirage 2000N/ASMP	15	1 570	1 × 300 kt	TN8	115
Mirage IVp/ASMP	18	1 500	1 × 300 kt	TN80	20
		(plus ASMP range of 80-250 km)			
Jaguar A	45	750	1 × 6-8/30 kt bomb	ant-52	50
Mirage IIIE	15	600	1 × 6-8/30 kt bomb	ant-52	35
Land missiles					
S3D	18	3 500	1 × 1 Mt	tn-61	18
Pluton	44	120	1 × 10/25 kt	ant-51	70
SLBMs					
M-20	64	3 000	1 × 1 Mt	tn-61	64
M-4A	16	4 000-5 000	6 × 150 kt (MIRV)	tn-70	96
M-4B	16	6 000	6 × 50 kt (MIRV)	tn-71	96

Land- and sea-based nuclear weapons [*continued*]

Weapon type	Number in service	Range (km)	Warhead load and yield	Warhead type	Number in the stockpile
Carrier aircraft					
Super Etendard	36	650	1 × 6-8/30 kt bomb	ant-52	40[j]

5. China

Aircraft					
B-5 (IL28)	15-30	1 850	1 × bomb (20 kt-3 Mt)		15-30
B-6 (Tu-16)	100	5 900	1-3 × bomb (20 kt-3 Mt)		100-130
Land missiles					
DF-2(CSS-1)	30-50	1 450	1 × 20 kt		30-50
DF-3(CSS-2)	75-100	2 600	1 × 1-3 Mt		75-100
DF-4(CSS-3)	~10	4 800-7 000	1 × 1-3 Mt		~10
DF-5(CSS-4)	~10	13 000	1 × 4-5 Mt		~10
SLBMs					
CSS-N-3 (JL-1)	24	3 300	1 × 200 kt-1 Mt		26-38[k]

a. All data on United States strategic forces from *SIPRI Yearbook 1989*, p. 12.
b. Thomas B. Cochran *et al.*, eds., *Nuclear Weapons Databook Vol. I: United States Nuclear Forces and Capabilities*, Cambridge, Mass. Ballinger, 1984, pp. 41-79. The variants also differ in the types of PALs.
c. The "numbers in service" refers to the total number of aircraft with nuclear capability in the United States arsenal. The range refers to the minimum and maximum range for this group of aircraft.
d. This number is the total number of nuclear-capable carrier aircraft in the United States Navy.
e. *SIPRI Yearbook 1989*, p. 13. Cochran, *op. cit.*, pp. 205-210, 213-223 and 232.
f. Data from Soviet official submission to the study and *SIPRI Yearbook 1989*, p. 14.
g. Data on Blackjack from Institute for Defense and Disarmament Studies (IDDS), *Arms Control Reporter 1989*, Brookline, IDDS, 1989, p. 611.E.1. Other data from *SIPRI Yearbook 1989*, p. 15.
h. Data on theatre forces from *SIPRI Yearbook 1989*, pp. 16 and 17.
i. British data from *SIPRI Yearbook 1989*, p. 18.
j. *SIPRI Yearbook 1989*, p. 19.
k. *Ibid.*, p. 20.

Group of experts

Ambassador Mohamed El-Shaffei Abdel Hamid
Former Under-Secretary of State
Ministry of Foreign Affairs
Cairo, Egypt

Mr. Gustavo Ainchil
General Department of International Security
and Strategic Affairs
Ministry of Foreign Affairs and Worship
Buenos Aires, Argentina

Mr. Alexander Akalovsky
Bureau of Multilateral Affairs
United States Arms Control and Disarmament Agency
Washington, DC, United States of America

Monsieur Gilles Curien
Ambassadeur de France
Ministère des Affairs Etrangères
Paris, France

Dr. Radoslav Deyanov
Advisor on Disarmament Matters
Ministry of Foreign Affairs
Sofia, Bulgaria

Dr. Hedy Hernández
Minister Counsellor
Department of International Politics
Department of Multilateral Affairs
Ministry of External Relations
Caracas, Venezuela

Ambassador Brett Lineham
High Commissioner
New Zealand High Commission
Tarawa, Kiribati

Mr. H. M. G. S. Palihakkara
First Secretary
Permanent Mission of Sri Lanka to the
United Nations Office at Geneva
Geneva, Switzerland

Ambassador Nana Sutresna
Ambassador Extraordinary and Plenipotentiary
Permanent Mission of Indonesia to the United Nations
New York, United States of America

Mr. Cheikh Sylla
Technical Counsellor
Ministère des Affairs Etrangères
Dakar, Senegal

Ambassador Maj Britt Theorin
Chairman of the Swedish Disarmament Delegation
Ministry of Foreign Affairs
Stockholm, Sweden

Professor Henry A. Trofimenko
Chief Analyst
Institute of United States and Canadian Studies
Academy of Sciences of the Union of
Soviet Socialist Republics
Moscow, Union of Soviet Socialist Republics

40267–December 1991–5,000